The Microwave *Diet* Cookbook

Jane Hunter

© 1994 The Magni Group, Inc.
Printed in USA

*Dedicated to Marty, my husband, for his kindness,
support, and sense of humor.*

ISBN 1-882330-22-6
© 1994 The Magni Group, Inc.
All rights reserved.
Published in the United States by The Magni Group, Inc.
P.O. Box 849 McKinney TX 75069

Printed in USA

Contents

Appetizers

Start off your meal with any of these low-fat, easy recipes.
Dining in courses allows you to eat slower, enjoying each part of
your meal, and leaves time for the "I've had enough" message to
get through.

Breakfast and Brunch

Whether you are on the go, or at your leisure, you'll find something tempting to wake up to. From the Cream Cheese and Fruit
Pita you can eat in the car, to a breakfast in bed of Strawberries,
French Toast and Cottage Cheese, you'll find it here.

Light Meals and Sandwiches

In the mood for something light? Choose one of these whole-some, delicious mini-meals. Team a sandwich with any of the following soup recipes and you have an American Classic lunch.

Soups

A comfort food and a wonderful low-calorie food. High in water content, and with an almost limitless variety of flavors, textures and colors. From the Shrimp Soup with Red Beans and Rice, to the Hearty Minestrone, enjoy any of these easy, nourishing soups.

Salads

Advice on healthy eating from the U.S. Department of Agriculture and Department of Health and Human Services: Eat a variety of foods, and choose a diet with plenty of vegetables, fruits and grain products. These American Regional and International Salads fulfill both requirements.

Vegetables

Now elevated in status in the balanced diet plan. Low in calories and high in fiber, vegetables are recognized for reducing the risk of leading life-threatening diseases. The complex carbohydrates in vegetables provide steady fuel for most of our body's functions. Enjoy sampling these creative selections.

Rice, Beans, Grains

Rice, beans, and grains have supplanted meat and dairy products in importance in a balanced, healthy diet. Try the Vegetable Paella, the Pureed Black Beans with Green chile, or the Green Bean Wild Rice for satisfying, flavorful food.

Pasta

Pasta can be filling without being fattening. The secret is in the sauce. Tomato Mushroom Sauce with Spiral Pasta, Asian Broccoli and Snow Pea Pasta, Linguine with Zucchini and Tomatoes, Spaghetti with Wild Mushrooms—the possibilities are only limited by your imagination.

Seafood

Fish and shellfish cook quickly and beautifully in the microwave oven. No need to fry in oil. Perfect for busy weight watchers. Pair one of the savory sauces in this book with simply cooked fish for sensational results.

Poultry

Poultry is economical, a good source of protein, and with the skin removed, it's low in calories and cholesterol. And, it's now no longer necessary to buy a whole turkey. Most markets offer turkey parts and ground turkey. Microwaving is an easy way to prepare poultry, easy on clean-up too, so enjoy the many recipes provided.

Meats

We are advised by nutritional experts to cut down on our consumption of meats, to eat smaller portions and to have fewer portions per week. It's good advice. These dishes call for lean cuts of meat, well trimmed of fat, and extra-lean ground meat. When you enjoy meat, you'll get protein, iron, zinc, B vitamins and other valuable nutrients.

Sauces, Dips and Spreads

Sauces, dips and spreads provide variety and excitement. Ones included in this book turn raw vegetables and bread into company food, baked potatoes into scrumptious feasts, and simply cooked fish and chicken into gourmet fare.

Desserts

How can desserts be good for you? From the Apple Crisp to the Special Bread Pudding and the Warm Fruit Medley, these desserts are low in sugar and fat and simple to prepare. Enjoy!

Snacks and Drinks

Say good-bye to sodas, candy, chips, and coffee. They're loaded with salt, sugar, fat and caffeine. They offer little, if any, real nutrition. Instead try Nachos, Applesauce Raisin Muffins, or Warmed Apple-Cranberry Juice.

Introduction

Cooking with the Microwave Diet Cookbook is easy, and there's no need to count calories. All the traditional and new recipes have been pared down to the minimum in calories, cholesterol, sugar, and salt, and high fat ingredients have been replaced by those with a low fat content. Enjoy!

Benefits of Microwave Cooking

The microwave cooks most foods more quickly than conventional methods. It exudes more fat from meats, leaving them healthier for you, and vegetables cook in their own juices, so that important vitamins aren't poured down the drain. Food doesn't stick to the pan, so less oil is used in cooking. Vegetables are perfectly suited for the microwave oven. It's a great tool for defrosting and indispensable for warming-up foods.

Conventional methods are more reliable for a few foods, like baked goods and cooked pasta. No problem! While the noodles are cooking on the stove top, or the bread is baking in the oven, you can use your microwave to create wonderful vegetables, sauces, meats and fish.

Current Nutritional Recommendations

Here are the seven dietary guidelines published in 1990 by the U.S. Department of Agriculture, and the Department of Health and Human Services:

- Eat a variety of foods.
- Maintain a healthy weight.
- Choose a diet low in fat, saturated fat, and cholesterol.
- Choose a diet with plenty of vegetables, fruits and grain products.
- Use sugars only in moderation.
- If you drink alcoholic beverages do so in moderation

The recipes in this book provide variety, are low in sugar, fat, cholesterol, sodium and calories. They provide plenty of interest and eye-appeal, and there is a large selection of vegetable, grain and fruit recipes to choose from. So eat and enjoy.

General Information for Using the Recipes

All recipes have been developed for a 650-700 watt microwave oven.

Use only microwave-safe glass and plastic plates, pans and accessories in your microwave oven.

All recipes are based on servings for four unless otherwise stated.

When a recipe says to cover, use the lid that goes with the casserole dish, or cover with microwaveable plastic wrap and slightly fold back wrap on one side, to vent.

Be careful when removing lids or plastic wrap from cooked foods. The pan sides may not feel hot, yet the escaping steam may burn you.

Jane Hunter

Jane Hunter grew up in the Midwest and received a B.A. in education from Michigan State University. Her life and career then transitioned to the Southern California area, where she pursued teaching for ten years. Recently, her interests have focused on entrepreneurship, painting, and delightfully healthful cooking, which resulted in this cookbook. "I love healthy delicious food—eating it, and making it for others, especially my husband, Marty, who can't get enough of it." This is her second cookbook.

APPETIZERS

Artichoke Stuffed Mushrooms

> 8 large or 12 medium-sized fresh mushrooms
> 1 (6-ounce) jar artichoke hearts, chopped
> 2 Tablespoons chopped pimiento
> 2 Tablespoons wine
> 1/2 teaspoon lemon juice
> 1/8 teaspoon black pepper
> dash cayenne pepper
> 1/2 teaspoon garlic powder
> 2 Tablespoons Parmesan cheese

Remove mushroom caps from stems and chop stems. Combine stems, artichoke hearts, pimiento, wine, lemon juice, peppers and garlic powder in a medium bowl. Microwave on HIGH for 2-3 minutes or until vegetables are tender-crisp, stirring twice.

Fill mushroom caps with mixture and sprinkle with Parmesan cheese. Place mushrooms on a large plate covered with two layers of paper towels. Microwave on HIGH for 2-3 minutes.

Marinated Mixed Vegetables

Easy and delicious.

> 1/2 red bell pepper, chopped into 1-inch pieces
> 1/2 green bell pepper, chopped into 1-inch pieces
> 1/2 cup low-fat salad dressing with herbs
> 1 Tablespoon Worcestershire sauce
> 1/2 pound mushrooms
> 10 cherry tomatoes
> 1 (8 1/2-ounce dry weight) jar artichoke hearts

Place bell pepper in a 2-quart dish. Cover and cook on HIGH for 1-2 minutes. Add remaining ingredients. Stir. Cover and marinate at room temperature for 30 minutes, stirring twice.

Before serving, cook covered vegetables and marinade on HIGH for 3-4 minutes.

Crab Stuffed Tomatoes

     4 medium tomatoes
     1/2 pound imitation crab meat
     3 finely chopped green onions
     1/4 cup finely chopped green pepper
     8 pitted ripe olives, chopped
     2 Tablespoons seasoned bread crumbs
     1 teaspoon red wine vinegar
     1/2 teaspoon parsley flakes

Cut stem end from tomatoes and create a cavity for filling. Set aside. In a small bowl, combine remaining ingredients. Stuff tomatoes.

Place tomatoes on plate covered with 2 layers of paper towel. Microwave on HIGH for 2-4 minutes until heated through, rotating plate halfway through cooking time.

Cajun Shrimp

     1 (10-ounce) package frozen medium-size cleaned
       shrimp, defrosted
     1 large clove garlic, crushed or minced
     1 small bay leaf
     3/4 teaspoons chili powder
     1/4 teaspoon dried oregano
     1/4 teaspoon celery seeds
     1/4 teaspoon paprika
     dash cayenne pepper

Rinse and drain shrimp. Combine all ingredients in a 2 1/2-quart casserole dish. Cover with wax paper and microwave on HIGH for 3-5 minutes until shrimp are opaque, stirring each one minute and removing any smaller shrimp that are done more quickly.

Chinese Shrimp

1 (10-ounce) package medium-size frozen cleaned
  shrimp, defrosted
1/2 Tablespoons fresh grated ginger or 1/2 teaspoon
  dried ginger.
1 large clove garlic, crushed or minced
1 Tablespoon lite soy sauce
1/8 cup rice wine vinegar

Rinse and drain shrimp. Combine all ingredients in a 2-quart
casserole dish. Cover with wax paper and microwave on HIGH
for 3-5 minutes, until shrimp are opaque, stirring each one
minute and removing any smaller shrimp that are done more
quickly.

Oriental Chicken and Vegetable Kabobs

12 wooden skewers, 6-inches long
1 whole boneless chicken breast, skinned, cut into 3/4
  inch pieces
1 large yellow onion, cut into 3/4 inch chunks
1 large green bell pepper, cut into 3/4-inch chunks
1 cup sliced water chestnuts
1/4 cup Teriyaki sauce
1 teaspoon lemon juice

Combine all ingredients in a shallow dish and cover. Marinate in
refrigerator for 1/2 hour. On each skewer alternate one piece of
chicken, onion, pepper and water chestnut.

Place filled skewers in a shallow baking dish or on a
microwaveable platter. Sprinkle with lemon juice. Cover with
wax paper and microwave on MEDIUM for 8-12 minutes until
chicken tests done, rearranging once.

Oriental Meatballs

Meatballs
1/2 pound ground turkey
1/2 teaspoon ground ginger
1/2 teaspoon garlic powder
3 Tablespoons fresh cilantro, chopped or 3 Tablespoons chopped green onion
2 Tablespoons sesame seeds
1/4 cup liquid egg substitute

Sauce
1/4 cup water
1/2 teaspoon cornstarch
2 Tablespoons lite Teriyaki sauce
1 teaspoon lemon juice

In a medium-size bowl, mix together meatball ingredients. Form meatballs using 2 teaspoons of meat mixture for each. Place meatballs in a shallow baking dish. Leave uncovered and cook on HIGH for 3-5 minutes until no longer pink, rearranging once. Remove from dish and set aside.

Pour sauce ingredients into meat juices in bottom of baking dish. Stir well. Microwave on HIGH for 2 1/2- 3 minutes until bubbly, stirring twice.

Pour sauce over meatballs, microwave on HIGH for 2 minutes to heat through.

Italian Potato Skins

serves 6

> 3 (5-ounce) baking potatoes, pierced
> 1 Tablespoon olive oil
> 1/4 teaspoon dried oregano
> 1 clove garlic, crushed
> 1/2 cup low-fat mozzarella cheese, shredded
> 3 green onions, diced

Arrange potatoes in oven with space around each. Microwave on HIGH for 7-9 minutes, turning over and rearranging after 4 minutes. Allow to cool. Cut in half lengthwise. Scoop flesh out of each half, leaving a 1/4-inch thick shell. (Save scooped-out potato for other uses. Set shells aside.

In a small bowl, mix oil, oregano and garlic. Brush on both sides of potato skins. Arrange skins in a circle on a plate with cut sides down. Cook on HIGH for 3-4 minutes. Turn skins over and sprinkle with cheese and onions. Reduce heat to MEDIUM HIGH (70% power) and cook for 1 minute until cheese is melted.

Celery Stuffed with Cheese and Vegetables

serves 10

> 5 celery stalks, trimmed
> 1 small onion, diced
> 1/2 green bell pepper
> 1/2 carrot
> 2 ounces low-fat cream cheese or Neufchatel cheese
> 1 teaspoon salt-free seasoning
> dash paprika

Place onion in a medium bowl. Cover and cook on HIGH for 2 minutes until soft. Finely chop bell pepper and carrot in a food processor. Add to onions. Add cream cheese and seasoning to onion mixture. Microwave on MEDIUM (50% power) for 30 seconds to soften cheese and mix well.

Spread cheese mixture into celery. Sprinkle with paprika. Cut each celery stalk into 4 pieces.

Eggplant Dip

yields 2 cups

Serve with French bread, crackers or raw vegetables.

1 medium eggplant, pierced several times with a fork
1 medium tomato, chopped
1 medium red onion, finely chopped
2 cloves garlic, minced
1 Tablespoon olive oil
2 Tablespoons fresh lemon juice
1/2 teaspoon sugar
2 Tablespoons fresh chopped cilantro
dash salt
dash pepper

Place eggplant on paper towel and microwave on HIGH for 6-8 minutes until softened. Allow to cool, then cut eggplant in half lengthwise and spoon out pulp into the container of a blender or food processor. Discard peel. Puree eggplant. Add remaining ingredients and mix well. Transfer to serving bowl and chill until serving time.

Marinated Vegetables

1/2 cup boiling water
1/2 teaspoon beef bouillon granules
1/4 cup white wine
1/4 teaspoon dried basil
1/4 teaspoon parsley flakes
1 bay leaf
2 small zucchini cut into 1-inch pieces
1 medium green pepper seeded and cut into 1-inch pieces
16 small fresh mushrooms
8 cherry tomatoes

In glass measure, combine boiling water and bouillon. Stir in wine and seasonings. Place vegetables in shallow baking dish. Pour broth over vegetables. Cover dish and let stand in refrigerator 1 to 2 hours, turning vegetables once or twice.

Discard marinade. Microwave vegetables on HIGH for 4-6 minutes, until tender-crisp. Stir after half the time.

Chicken-Stuffed Mushrooms

> **16 medium-sized mushrooms**
> **1/4 cup celery, diced**
> **1 green onion, chopped**
> **1/8 teaspoon black pepper**
> **1/4 cup green bell pepper, diced**
> **1/2 cup chopped cooked chicken**
> **1/4 cup low-fat cheddar cheese**

Wash and pat dry mushrooms. Remove stems and reserve for another use.

In a small bowl combine celery, onion, black pepper and bell pepper. Cover and microwave on HIGH for 1-2 minutes. Drain. Stir chicken and cheese into vegetable mixture.

Fill each mushroom cap with the chicken mixture and arrange on a large microwaveable plate. Microwave on HIGH for 2-3 minutes until heated through, rotating plate a half turn once, and removing any smaller mushrooms as soon as they are done.

Warm Tuna Crudites

makes 24

> **1 (3-ounce) package low-fat Neufchatel cheese**
> **1/4 cup chopped green onions**
> **1 Tablespoon skim milk**
> **2 Tablespoons fresh diced parsley**
> **1/2 teaspoon dried dill weed**
> **1 teaspoon lemon juice**
> **1 (6 1/2-ounce) can water packed tuna, drained**
> **1 large zucchini cut into 1/2-inch rounds**
> **1 large yellow bell pepper cut into 1 1/2-inch triangles**
> **paprika to garnish**

In a medium bowl, combine cheese, milk, onions, parsley, dill, and lemon juice. Add tuna and mix well. Arrange vegetables on a large microwaveable plate and spoon mixture onto each piece.

Sprinkle with paprika and microwave on MEDIUM LOW (30% power) just until warm.

Savory Cheese Crackers

> 1 (3-ounce) package low-fat cream cheese
> 1/4 cup chopped green onions
> 1 Tablespoon diced pimiento
> 1/2 teaspoon garlic powder
> 1/4 teaspoon sesame seeds
> 20 whole wheat fat-free onion crackers

Microwave cheese on MEDIUM LOW (30% power) in a small bowl for 1 minutes until soft. Add onions, pimiento, garlic powder and sesame seeds, mixing well.

Spread 1 teaspoon of the cheese mixture on each cracker and place about 10 crackers on a plate. Microwave first filled plate on MEDIUM (50% power) for 1 minute until warm. Repeat with remaining crackers.

Mock Fried Zucchini

serves 16

> 1/3 cup olive oil
> 1/2 cup bread crumbs
> 1 teaspoon garlic powder
> 1 teaspoon dried basil
> 1 teaspoon parsley flakes
> 1/4 teaspoon dried oregano
> 3 medium zucchini, cut in 1/2 x 2-inch strips

Place olive oil in a small bowl. Place bread crumbs, garlic powder, basil, parsley and paprika in a plastic bag. Dip zucchini in oil, then shake in crumb mixture to coat.

Arrange zucchini on a microwaveable rack. Cover with wax paper and microwave on HIGH for 2 minutes.

Rearrange by moving inside pieces to outside of dish. Re-cover and microwave on HIGH for 1-3 minutes until heated through.

Liver Pate

Serve with raw vegetables, your favorite crackers, or spoon onto fresh French bread.

> 1 pound chicken livers
> 1 small chopped onion
> 3 small cloves garlic, minced
> 1 Tablespoon white wine
> 1/2 teaspoon parsley flakes
> 1/4 teaspoon pepper

Rinse and drain livers. Combine livers, onion, garlic, wine and seasonings in 2-quart casserole dish. Cover and cook on HIGH 5-8 minutes until tested done.

Place cooked liver mixture in blender or food processor. Process until smooth. Put in serving dish and chill.

Salmon Spread

Serve with fat-free whole wheat crackers.

> 1 (16-ounce) can salmon, drained, flaked, bones and
>   skin removed
> 4 ounces low-fat cream cheese
> 2 teaspoons lemon juice
> 2 teaspoons Dijon mustard
> 1 Tablespoon rinsed and drained capers
> 2 Tablespoons chopped pimiento
> 2 Tablespoons snipped parsley
> 1 Tablespoon snipped chives
> 1 Tablespoon minced onion

Place cream cheese in mixing bowl and microwave on HIGH for 30 seconds until soft. Flake salmon into cream cheese. Stir in remaining ingredients. Refrigerate. Serve with fat-free whole wheat crackers.

Walnut Stuffed Mushrooms

      15-20 large mushrooms
      1/4 cup finely chopped onion
      1 Tablespoon olive oil
      1/2 cup bread crumbs
      1/4 cup chopped walnuts
      1 Tablespoon parsley flakes
      1 Tablespoon chopped pimiento
      1/2 teaspoon pepper

Pull stems out of mushrooms creating cavity. Chop stems to make 1 cup and combine chopped stems, onions and oil in a medium bowl. Cook on HIGH for 2-3 minutes until mushrooms are soft. Add bread crumbs, nuts, parsley, pimiento, and pepper. Stir. Stuff each mushroom. Arrange on large tray lined with paper towel. Cover with wax paper and microwave on HIGH for 3-4 minutes until mushrooms are slightly soft to the touch.

Warmed Crab-Curry Dip

Serve with your favorite crackers or raw vegetables.

      1 Tablespoon margarine
      1/2 teaspoon curry powder
      1 Tablespoon all-purpose flour
      3/4 cup skim milk
      1 1/2 cups flaked fresh crab meat, or imitation crab
        meat
      1/4 teaspoon celery seed
      1/4 teaspoon garlic powder
      1/4 teaspoon onion powder
      1/8 teaspoon red pepper

In glass measure, melt margarine on HIGH for 30 seconds. Add curry and flour and whisk until smooth. Whisk in milk. Microwave on HIGH for 2-3 minutes, until thickened and smooth, whisking every minute. Combine crab and spices in a small casserole dish. Pour sauce over crab and mix together. Cover and microwave on MEDIUM (50% power) for 5-6 minutes until hot, stirring twice.

Marinated Mushrooms

  1/2 cup water
  1/4 cup red wine vinegar
  1/2 teaspoon sugar
  1 Tablespoon olive oil
  1/4 cup finely minced onion
  1 clove garlic, finely minced
  1/4 teaspoon dried oregano
  1/4 teaspoon dried basil
  1/8 teaspoon paprika
  1/8 teaspoon red pepper
  2 medium yellow crookneck squash, cut into 1-inch
  cubes
  1 pound small fresh mushrooms, uniformly sized

Combine all ingredients except mushrooms in 2-quart casserole
dish. Cover and microwave on HIGH for 3-4 minutes. Add
mushrooms and microwave on MEDIUM HIGH (70% power)
for 3-4 minutes until mushrooms are tender, stirring every 2
minutes. Refrigerate for 6-8 hours. Drain off liquids and serve
with toothpicks.

BREAKFAST AND BRUNCH

Black Bean Scrambled Eggs

> 1 cup liquid egg substitute
> 1/2 cup shredded fat-free jack cheese
> 1/2 cup green pepper, diced
> 1/2 cup cooked black beans
> 1 small onion, diced
> dash black pepper
> 1 small tomato, diced for garnish

Combine all ingredients except tomato in casserole dish.
Microwave on MEDIUM HIGH (70% power) for 5-7 minutes,
stirring each 1 minute. When done eggs should still look wet. Let
stand 1 minute and garnish with tomato.

Bell Pepper and Zucchini Breakfast Burrito

> 1/2 small green bell pepper, sliced into thin 2-inch long
>   strips
> 1/2 small red bell pepper, sliced into thin 2-inch long
>   strips
> 1/2 small zucchini, sliced into thin 2-inch long strips
> 1/2 teaspoon garlic powder
> 1/8 teaspoon parsley flakes
> 1 cup liquid egg substitute
> 4 flour or corn tortillas

Place bell peppers and zucchini in a small bowl, cover and cook
on HIGH for 2-3 minutes until tender-crisp. Let stand, covered
for 3 minutes.

Mix herbs and egg substitute in a small bowl. Cook on MEDIUM
HIGH (70% power for 4-6 minutes until eggs are almost dry.

Spoon mixture onto tortillas and top with vegetable slices. Roll
tortillas and place seam side down, edges not touching, in a
baking dish. Microwave on MEDIUM for 1-2 minutes until
tortillas are hot.

'Grilled' Potatoes

> 2 teaspoons soft-spread margarine
> 1 small onion, diced
> 1 green onion, finely chopped
> 1/2 teaspoon browning sauce
> 1/2 garlic powder
> 1/4 teaspoon basil
> 2 medium baking potatoes, peeled and cut into 1/2-inch cubes

Combine margarine, onion, green onion, browning sauce, garlic powder and basil in a casserole dish. Microwave on HIGH for 15-20 seconds until margarine is melted.

Add potatoes and coat with margarine mixture. Cook on HIGH for 7-9 minutes until potatoes are fork-tender, stirring every 2 minutes.

Warmed Grapefruit with Berries

> 2 grapefruit, sliced in half, sections loosened
> 3 Tablespoons unsweetened raspberry fruit spread
> 1/2 cup raspberries or blueberries

Spread tops of grapefruits with raspberry spread. Microwave on HIGH for 2 minutes. Rotate grapefruits 1/2 turn and microwave an additional 2-4 minutes until hot throughout. Garnish with fresh raspberries or blueberries and serve.

Cheddar Cheese Scrambled Eggs

> 1 cup liquid egg substitute
> 1/2 cup shredded fat-free cheddar cheese
> 1/2 green bell pepper, diced
> 1/4 teaspoon garlic powder
> 1/4 cup chopped green onion
> 1 dash black pepper
> 1 Tablespoon pimento, chopped

Combine all ingredients in medium casserole. Microwave on MEDIUM HIGH (70% power) for 5-7 minutes, stirring each 1 minute. When done, eggs should still look wet. Let stand 1 minute.

Banana Nut Muffins

> 3/4 cup whole wheat baking mix
> 1/4 teaspoon baking soda
> 1 Tablespoon sugar
> 1/4 teaspoon ground cinnamon
> 1/3 cup mashed ripe banana
> 3 Tablespoons skim milk
> 1/4 cup liquid egg substitute or 1 egg
> 1/4 cup chopped walnuts

> Topping
> 2 Tablespoons sugar
> 1 teaspoon cinnamon
> 1 Tablespoon finely chopped walnuts

Line 7 custard cups with paper baking cups. In a 4-cup microwaveable measure combine baking mix, baking soda, sugar, and cinnamon. Stir. Add banana, milk, egg and nuts. Stir well. Fill baking cups half full.

In another custard cup, mix together topping ingredients. Sprinkle evenly over unbaked muffins. Arrange muffins in a ring in microwave oven and cook on HIGH for 1 minute. Rotate cups 1/2 turn. Cook another 1-2 minutes on HIGH until tops spring back when lightly touched. Remove immediately from custard cups to wire rack. Let cool.

Potato and 'Sausage' Breakfast Casserole

1/2 package (8-ounces) turkey breakfast sausage
3 small thin-skinned potatoes, sliced
2 green onions, finely chopped
1/4 teaspoon dried basil
dash black pepper

Crumble sausage into casserole dish. Stir in remaining ingredients. Cover and cook on HIGH for 6-8 minutes, stirring each 2 minutes until potatoes are fork-tender.

French Toast

serves 2

1/2 cup liquid egg substitute (or 2 eggs)
1/4 teaspoon vanilla extract
1 Tablespoon skim milk
1/2 teaspoon ground cinnamon
2 slices whole wheat bread

Whisk together egg substitute, milk, vanilla and cinnamon in shallow bowl. Dip bread slices in mixture. Coat well. Turn over and let soak 1 minute.

Place both bread slice on microwaveable platter. Microwave on MEDIUM HIGH (70% power) for 2 minutes.

Turn bread over and microwave an additional 1 1/2 - 2 minutes until bread is dry to the touch. Serve with maple syrup if desired.

Strawberry French Toast with Cottage Cheese

1/4-1/2 cup fat-free cottage cheese
1/4-1/2 cup sliced strawberries *or*
3 Tablespoons strawberry fruit spread.

Follow recipe for French toast. When French toast has finished cooking, spread each slice with cottage cheese and top with strawberries or fruit spread. Microwave on HIGH for 1 minute to warm through.

Mushroom Egg Burritos

> **1 cup liquid egg substitute**
> **1 small onion chopped**
> **1/4 cup chopped green bell pepper**
> **8 ounces sliced fresh mushrooms**
> **4 corn or flour tortillas**
> **1/4 cup shredded low-fat jack cheese**

Combine egg substitute, onion, bell pepper and mushrooms in shallow baking dish. Microwave on MEDIUM (70% power) for 5-7 minutes until eggs are almost dry, stirring 3 times.

Spoon egg mixture onto tortillas, add 1 Tablespoon cheese, roll up and place seam side down, burritos not touching each other, on platter. Sprinkle remaining cheese on top. Microwave on MEDIUM (50% power) for 1-2 minutes to melt cheese and heat tortillas.

Cheese and 'Sausage' Strata

serves 6

> **1/2 package turkey sausage (8-ounces)**
> **3/4 cup liquid egg substitute**
> **1 1/4 cups skim milk**
> **2 teaspoons Dijon-style mustard**
> **4 slices whole wheat bread, cubed**
> **3/4 cup low-fat Swiss cheese**
> **1 Tablespoon parsley flakes**
> **1/2 teaspoon dried chives**
> **dash ground nutmeg**
> **12 apples—sliced, brushed with lemon for garnish**

Spread turkey sausage in baking dish, cover, and cook on HIGH for 3-5 minutes, stirring twice to crumble. Drain and set aside.

Coat a 1 1/2-quart casserole dish with cooking spray. Place cubed bread evenly over bottom of dish. Spread sausage evenly over bread. Sprinkle with cheese, parsley and chives on top. In a 4-cup microwaveable measure, combine egg substitute, mustard and milk. Pour over bread, sausage and cheese mixture. Cover and let stand for 5 minutes. Uncover and microwave on MEDIUM HIGH (70% power) for 10-15 minutes or until set. Top with apple slices. Let stand 3 minutes.

Cinnamon Raisin Applesauce

> 2 cups unsweetened applesauce
> 1/4 cup raisins
> ground cinnamon to taste

Combine applesauce and raisins in casserole. Cover and microwave on HIGH for 2-4 minutes until heated through. Sprinkle cinnamon on top and serve.

Scrambled Eggs Durango

> 1 cup liquid egg substitute
> 1/4 cup chopped green bell pepper
> 2 green onions, chopped
> 1/4 cup crookneck squash, chopped
> 1 small tomato, chopped
> 1/4 teaspoon parsley flakes
> 1/4 teaspoon dried oregano
> 1/8 teaspoon black pepper
> 1/4 cup shredded fat-free mozzarella cheese

Combine all ingredients except cheese in casserole dish. Microwave on MEDIUM HIGH (70% power) for 5-7 minutes, stirring each 1 minute. When done, eggs should be set but still moist. Mix in cheese and allow to stand, covered for 1 minute to melt cheese.

Blueberry Cream Cheese Bagels

> 6 Tablespoon fat-free cream cheese
> 4 teaspoons chopped walnuts
> 2 bagels, cut in half, toasted
> 1 cup fresh blueberries, or other berries

In a small bowl, soften cheese on MEDIUM LOW (30% power) for 1 minute. Blend in nuts. Spread cheese mixture on each bagel half. Top each with berries.

Broccoli and Turkey-Bacon Omelet

> **2 slices turkey-bacon, chopped**
> **1/2 cup broccoli, chopped**
> **1 small onion, chopped**
> **1 cup liquid egg substitute (or 4 eggs)**
> **1/2 teaspoon garlic powder**

Combine turkey-bacon, broccoli and onion in a 1 1/2 - quart casserole dish. Cover and cook on HIGH for 2-4 minutes until vegetables are tender-crisp. Drain.

Add eggs and garlic powder to broccoli mixture and stir. Cook on Medium High (70% power) for 3-5 minutes until eggs have set but are still moist. Let stand 1 minute.

Stewed Strawberries and Rhubarb

> **1 (20-ounce) package frozen rhubarb (about 4 cups)**
> **1/4 cup apple juice**
> **2 cups fresh sliced strawberries**
> **2 Tablespoons honey**
> **1/2 teaspoon cinnamon**

Combine rhubarb, apple juice and cinnamon in casserole dish. Cover and microwave on HIGH for 11-13 minutes until rhubarb is tender, stirring every 3 minutes. Slightly mash rhubarb, add strawberries and honey. Microwave on MEDIUM (50% power) for 1 minute to heat strawberries through.

Cream Cheese and Fruit Pita

Easy to handle when eating on the run

> **2 6-inch pita breads**
> **4 Tablespoons fat-free cream cheese**
> **4 Tablespoons chopped walnuts**
> **1 cup sliced strawberries**
> **1/4 teaspoon cinnamon**
> **1/8 teaspoon nutmeg**

Slice pita breads in half and fill each with cheese, walnuts and strawberries. Place on a plate covered with 2 layers of paper towels. Cover with paper towel and microwave on HIGH for 45 seconds to 1 1/2 minutes to warm. Sprinkle with nutmeg and cinnamon.

Scrambled Eggs and 'Sausage'

> 1 cup liquid egg substitute
> 1 small onion, chopped
> 1/4 green bell pepper, diced
> 1/2 pound turkey sausage
> 1 small tomato, chopped for garnish
> 8 pitted black olives, sliced for garnish

Combine egg substitute, onion, bell pepper and sausage in a casserole dish. Microwave on MEDIUM HIGH (70% power) for 6-8 minutes until turkey is done and eggs are almost dry, stirring each 1 minute. Garnish with tomatoes and olives and serve.

Breakfast Omelet

> 3 slices turkey bacon, chopped
> 1/2 cup chopped green onions
> 1 cup sliced fresh mushrooms
> 1 cup liquid egg substitute
> 1/4 teaspoon dried basil
> 1/8 teaspoon dried oregano
> 1/4 cup fat-free Cheddar Cheese
> 1 small tomato, seeded and chopped

Place turkey-bacon on a paper plate, and cover with a paper towel. Microwave on HIGH for 2 minutes.

In a medium bowl, combine cooked turkey bacon, green onions and mushrooms. Microwave on HIGH for 3 minutes until mushrooms have softened, stirring once.

Add egg substitute, basil and oregano to bacon and mushroom mixture. Pour into a 9-inch microwaveable pie plate. Cook on MEDIUM (50% power) for 4-6 minutes until edges look slightly set, rotating dish once.

Carefully lift edges of omelet with a rubber spatula to allow uncooked egg to run underneath. Sprinkle with tomato and cheese. Microwave on MEDIUM an additional 3-5 minutes until set but still moist.

Summer Oatmeal

> 1 1/3 cups water
> 2/3 cup old fashioned oatmeal
> 1 Tablespoon maple syrup
> 1/2 orange, peeled and sectioned
> 1 1/2 Tablespoons chopped walnuts

Combine water, oatmeal and maple syrup in a bowl. Cook on HIGH for 3-4 minutes to desired consistency. Spoon into individual bowls, top with orange sections and walnuts, and serve.

Banana Oatmeal

serves 2

> 1 1/3 cups + 2 Tablespoons skim milk
> 2/3 cup old fashioned oatmeal
> 2 Tablespoons raisins
> 1 small banana, peeled and sliced
> 1/2 teaspoon cinnamon

Combine 1 1/3 cup milk, oatmeal, and raisins in a bowl. Cook on HIGH for 3-4 minutes to desired consistency. Stir in banana, cinnamon and 2 Tablespoons milk. Cook an additional 1 minute to heat through.

Apple Oatmeal

serves 2

> Oatmeal
> 1 cup water
> 1/3 cup apple juice
> 2/3 cup old fashioned oatmeal
>
> Topping
> 1/2 cup diced apple
> 1/4 teaspoon ground cinnamon
> dash nutmeg
> 1 teaspoon honey

Stir topping ingredients together in a casserole dish. Microwave on HIGH for 2 minutes until apple is tender, stirring once. Let stand covered.

Combine oatmeal ingredients in a bowl. Microwave on HIGH for 3-4 minutes to desired consistency. Top with cooked apple and serve.

Breakfast Quiche

> 1 (10-ounce) package frozen chopped spinach
> 1 small finely chopped onion
> 1 cup liquid egg substitute
> 1 cup low-fat ricotta cheese
> 4 medium mushrooms, finely sliced
> 1/4 teaspoon black pepper
> 1/4 teaspoon nutmeg
> 2 Tablespoons all-purpose flour
> 1/8 teaspoon paprika

Combine spinach and onion in a casserole dish. Cover and microwave on HIGH for 3 minutes. Stir, and cook an additional 3 minutes. Drain well. (Place in strainer. Press with a spoon.)

In a mixing bowl, beat egg substitute. Stir in cheese, mushrooms, pepper, nutmeg and flour. Stir in spinach and onion. Spread mixture evenly into a 9-inch microwaveable pie plate. Sprinkle with paprika.

Microwave on MEDIUM HIGH (70% power) for 6 minutes, rotating every 2 minutes. Reduce power to MEDIUM (50% power) and microwave an additional 5-10 minutes until center is set. Let stand 3 minutes.

Scrambled Egg Burritos

> 1 cup liquid egg substitute
> 1/4 cup chopped green onion
> 1/2 cup chopped bell pepper
> 1 small tomato, seeded and chopped
> 1/4 teaspoon garlic powder
> 1/8 teaspoon black pepper
> 4 flour or corn tortillas
> 1/4 cup low-fat Cheddar cheese, shredded

In a shallow baking dish, combine egg substitute, onion, bell pepper, tomato and spices. Cook on MEDIUM HIGH for 5-7 minutes until eggs are set but still moist, stirring twice.

Spoon egg mixture onto tortillas, add 1 Tablespoon cheese to each. Roll up and place seam side down on baking dish, topping with remaining cheese. Microwave on MEDIUM (50% power) for 1 minute to melt cheese and heat tortillas.

Breakfast Pita

> 4 slices turkey bacon
> 1 cup liquid egg substitute
> 1 small zucchini, diced
> 1/4 cup diced green onion
> 1/4 cup shredded fat-free Cheddar cheese
> 1/2 teaspoon garlic powder
> dash black pepper
> 2 6-inch pita breads

Place turkey bacon on two layers of paper towel in the microwave oven. Cover with another paper towel. Cook on HIGH for 3-3 1/3 minutes to desired crispness. Chop.

Combine turkey bacon, and remaining ingredients except pita breads, in a 2-quart casserole dish. Microwave on MEDIUM HIGH (70% power) for 5-7 minutes, stirring each 1 minute, until eggs are set but moist.

Wrap pita breads with paper towel. Microwave on HIGH for 45 seconds to heat throughout. Split and fill with egg mixture.

LIGHT MEALS AND SANDWICHES

Turkey Pita Pockets

> Sandwich
> 4 6-inch pita breads
> 1/2 bunch red leaf lettuce, washed
> 2 cups cooked turkey or chicken, sliced
>
> Yogurt Mustard Dressing
> 1/2 cup plain nonfat yogurt
> 2 Tablespoons Dijon mustard
> 1 medium tomato, chopped
> 1/4 teaspoon minced garlic
> 1/4 teaspoon pepper
> 1/4 teaspoon dill weed

Mix together Yogurt Mustard Dressing ingredients in a small bowl. Cover and microwave on MEDIUM LOW (30% power) for 2 minutes to warm, stirring twice. Place pita breads between 2 paper towels. Microwave on HIGH for 1 minute to heat through. Split bread and fill with turkey, lettuce and dressing.

Open Faced Vegetarian Sandwich

> 1/2 ripe avocado
> 1 Tablespoon water
> 1 teaspoon lemon juice
> 4 slices whole wheat bread, toasted
> 1/2 teaspoon onion powder
> 8 thin slices tomato
> 1 cup alfalfa sprouts
> 1 cucumber, thinly sliced
> 1/2 cup shredded fat-free Cheddar cheese

In a small bowl, mash avocado with water and lemon juice. Spread on each slice of toast. Sprinkle with onion powder and top with tomato slices, then sprouts, cucumber and cheese.

Place on a microwaveable platter lined with paper towels and microwave on MEDIUM (50% power) for 2 minutes to just melt cheese.

Turkey Melt Sandwich

> 2 Tablespoons low-fat mayonnaise or mayonnaise
>   substitute
> 1 teaspoon Dijon-style mustard
> 4 slices whole wheat bread, toasted
> 4 thin slices red onion
> 4 (1-ounce) slices turkey
> 1 cup alfalfa sprouts
> 4 (2/3-ounce) slices low-fat Swiss cheese, cut into long
>   strips

Combine mayonnaise and mustard in a small bowl. Spread on each slice of toast. Top with onion, turkey, sprouts and cheese.

Place on a microwaveable platter lined with paper towel. Microwave on MEDIUM (50% power) for 2 minutes until cheese just melts.

Barbecue Tofu and Bean Tacos

An excellent alternative to beef tacos.

> 2 teaspoons water
> 1 small onion, thinly sliced, rings separated
> 1 small green bell pepper, cut into thin 2-inch strips
> 1 pound firm tofu, crumbled
> 1 cup cooked beans
> 1 teaspoon chili powder
> 1 teaspoon cumin
> 3 Tablespoons barbecue sauce
> 8 (6-inch) corn tortillas
> 1 medium tomato, chopped, for garnish

Combine water, onion and pepper in dish. Cover and cook on HIGH for 3-4 minutes. Stir in tofu, chili powder, beans, cumin and barbecue sauce. Cover and cook on HIGH for 2-3 minutes to heat through.

Wrap tortillas in slightly damp paper towels and microwave on HIGH for 45 seconds to soften.

Fill tortillas with tofu mixture. Garnish with tomatoes. Fold over and serve.

Sautéed Mushrooms with Olives on Whole Wheat Rolls

> 4 large whole wheat rolls, sliced in half lengthwise
> 1 Tablespoon olive oil, divided
> 1 medium onion, thinly sliced, rings separated
> 8 ounces fresh sliced mushrooms
> 1 teaspoon lemon juice
> 1 Tablespoon low-fat mayonnaise or mayonnaise substitute
> 1 teaspoon Dijon-style mustard
> 1/2 cup alfalfa sprouts
> 8 Greek-style olives, pitted

Brush insides of rolls with half of the olive oil. Lay brushed sides down on a large frying pan over low heat to grill. Meanwhile, place remainder of the oil and the onion in a 2 1/2-quart casserole dish. Cover and microwave on HIGH for 3 minutes. Add mushrooms, re-cover, and cook on HIGH for 4-5 minutes until vegetables are soft. Stir in juice, mayonnaise and mustard. Spoon onto grilled rolls. Top with sprouts and olives.

Easy Rice and Bean Burrito

> 3/4 cup water
> 3/4 cup instant brown rice
> 3/4 cup vegetarian-style canned refried beans
> 1/3 cup salsa
> 1/2 cup low-fat Cheddar cheese, shredded
> 4 large tortillas

Combine water and rice in a 2-quart casserole dish. Cover and cook on HIGH for 6 minutes. Set aside. Place beans in a small bowl, stirring and pushing beans to the outside of the dish, forming a cavity in the center. Cover and microwave on HIGH for 1-2 minutes to heat through. Stir. Wrap tortillas in slightly damp paper towel and microwave on HIGH for 45 seconds to soften. Spread beans, rice, salsa and cheese on each tortilla. Roll up. Place seam side down on a baking dish, burritos not touching. Microwave an additional 1 minute on HIGH to warm through.

Steamed Vegetable Burrito

2 teaspoons olive oil
1 small zucchini, chopped
1 small onion, chopped
1 cup broccoli florets
1 cup cauliflower florets
1 teaspoon salt-free seasoning
dash black pepper
4 (6-inch) flour tortillas

Combine margarine, vegetables and seasoning in a 2-quart casserole dish. Cover and cook on HIGH for 6-7 minutes until vegetables are tender. Drain. Let stand covered.

Wrap tortillas in slightly damp paper towels. Microwave on HIGH for 45 seconds to soften. Spoon vegetable mixture into center of each tortilla and roll up.

Easy Sautéed Mushroom Burrito

4 (6-inch) flour tortillas
1 small onion chopped
8 ounces fresh mushrooms, sliced
1 teaspoon olive oil
1 cup cooked brown rice
1/8 teaspoon garlic powder (optional)
dash black pepper

Wrap tortillas in slightly damp paper towels and microwave on HIGH for 45 seconds to soften. Keep wrapped Place onion, mushrooms and oil in a 2-quart casserole dish. Cover and microwave on HIGH for 2 1/2 to 3 minutes until tender. Stir rice into mushroom mixture and cook an additional 2 minutes.

Spoon mushroom rice mixture onto tortillas. Sprinkle with garlic powder and pepper and roll up. Place seam side down on a baking dish, burritos not touching and microwave on HIGH for 1 minute to heat through.

Easy Turkey and Avocado Burritos

    4 (6-inch) flour tortillas
    2 cups cooked turkey, shredded
    1 ripe avocado, peeled, pitted and sliced
    1/2 cup grated low-fat Swiss cheese
    1/3 cup mild, chunky salsa

Wrap tortillas in slightly damp paper towels and microwave on HIGH for 45 seconds to soften.

Arrange turkey, avocado, cheese and salsa on each tortilla and roll up.

Arrange seam side down, space between each burrito, on a baking dish. Cover with wax paper and microwave on HIGH for 2-3 minutes until warmed through.

Creamy Chicken Pitas

    1/4 cup low-fat ricotta cheese
    3 Tablespoons finely chopped red onion
    1/2 cup finely chopped celery
    1/4 cup shredded carrot
    1/4 teaspoon garlic powder
    1 1/2 cups chopped cooked chicken
    2 pita breads, halved
    1 cup Romaine lettuce, torn
    1/3 cup seeded chopped tomato, for garnish
    dash pepper

In casserole dish, combine cheese, onion, celery, carrots, garlic powder, and chicken. Microwave on HIGH for 2-4 minutes to heat through, stirring twice.

Fit lettuce leaves into pita halves. Spoon in chicken mixture. Place sandwiches on large plate lined with a double layer of paper towel. Microwave on MEDIUM (50% power) for 1 1/2 minutes. Open sandwiches slightly and sprinkle with tomato and pepper.

Chicken Nuggets

> 2 boned skinned chicken breasts, cut into 1 1/2-inch
>   cubes
> 1 1/2 cups Italian-seasoned bread crumbs
> Barbecue or spaghetti sauce for dipping

Cover large microwaveable plate with 2 layers of paper towel.
Rinse chicken; do not pat dry.

Place bread crumbs in plastic bag. Add chicken cubes, a few at a
time, shaking to coat. Arrange chicken on towel covered plate.
Microwave on HIGH for 3 minutes. Rearrange, moving center
pieces to outside. Microwave on HIGH for 3-4 more minutes.
Serve with sauces.

Easy Mini Pizzas

> 2-3 English muffins
> 1/2 pound extra-lean ground beef
> 1/4 cup diced onion
> 1/4 cup diced green bell pepper
> 2/3 cup unsalted tomato sauce
> 1/3 cup grated low-fat Parmesan cheese
> 6 pitted ripe olives, chopped

In microwave-safe plastic colander, combine beef, onion and bell
pepper. Set in bowl. Microwave on HIGH for 3-4 minutes until
meat is no longer pink, stirring twice to break apart meat
chunks. Split muffins with fork. Place cut side up on a plate
covered with 2 paper towels. Onto each muffin half spoon
cooked ground meat mixture, tomato sauce, mozzarella cheese
and olives. Microwave on HIGH for 2-2 1/2 minutes until heated
through and cheese is melted.

Italian Hero Sandwiches

> 1/2 pound extra-lean ground beef
> 1/2 medium green bell pepper, chopped
> 1/4 cup chopped onions
> 1 cup mushroom spaghetti sauce
> 4 whole wheat hot dog buns, split
> 4 slices low-fat Swiss cheese, cut in halves

Combine beef, bell pepper and onion in microwaveable colander. Place colander in bowl. Microwave on HIGH for 3-4 minutes, until tested done, stirring twice to break apart meat chunks. In medium bowl, combine meat mixture and spaghetti sauce. Cover and microwave on HIGH for 2-3 minutes to heat through.

Open buns and remove some of each bun center to form a cavity for filling. Place cavity side up on microwaveable tray lined with 2 layers of paper towel. Fill with meat mixture. Top with cheese. Microwave on MEDIUM (50% power) for 2-3 minutes or until heated through.

Spinach Florentine Sandwiches

> 1 (10-ounce) package frozen chopped spinach
> 1 (4-ounce) carton low-fat ricotta cheese
> 1/4 teaspoon black pepper
> 2 English muffins, halved and toasted
> 4 very thin tomato slices
> 4 anchovy fillets, patted dry

Microwave frozen spinach in casserole dish on HIGH for 6 minutes, stirring after half the time. Drain thoroughly (place in strainer, press with spoon).

In casserole dish, mix together spinach, cheese and pepper. Heat on MEDIUM HIGH (70% power) for 2 minutes. Spoon over freshly toasted English muffins. Top with tomato and anchovy.

Sloppy Joes

> 3/4 pound lean ground sirloin
> 1 medium onion, diced
> 1/2 medium green bell pepper, diced
> 1 (8-ounce) can low-salt whole tomatoes, chopped with
>   their juice
> 1/4 cup fresh sliced mushrooms
> 1 teaspoon Worcestershire sauce
> 1/4 teaspoon dried basil
> 2 whole wheat hamburger buns, split
> 1/4 cup grated fat-free Cheddar cheese

Combine ground meat, onion and green pepper in plastic colander. Microwave on HIGH for 3-5 minutes until meat is no longer pink, stirring twice and breaking apart meat chunks.

In a casserole dish, mix together meat mixture, tomatoes, mushrooms, Worcestershire sauce and basil. Microwave on HIGH for 3-4 minutes until heated through and mushrooms have softened.

Spoon meat mixture evenly over bun halves. Sprinkle with cheese. Serve open faced.

Fat Free Quesadillas

> 1/2 cup shredded fat-free mozzarella cheese
> 1/2 cup shredded fat-free cheddar cheese
> 4 (6-inch) corn tortillas
> 2 Tablespoons salsa

Combine cheeses. Lay tortilla on a paper towel and sprinkle with 1/4 of cheeses. Top with 1/2 Tablespoons of salsa. Microwave on MEDIUM (50% power) for 1 minute until cheese is melted. Fold in half and repeat with remaining ingredients.

Turkey-Bacon, Lettuce and Tomato Sandwiches

serves 2

> 6 slices turkey bacon
> 6 fresh lettuce leaves
> 1/2 cup alfalfa sprouts
> 2 thick slices from large tomato
> 1/2 cucumber, sliced into 1/4-inch rounds
> 3 Tablespoons low-fat mayonnaise, or mayonnaise
>   substitute
> dash black pepper
> 4 slices whole-wheat bread, toasted

Arrange turkey-bacon on paper plate, cover with wax paper and cook on HIGH for 3 1/2-4 minutes, to desired crispness.

While turkey-bacon is cooking begin assembling sandwiches. Spread mayonnaise on one side of all four slices of bread. Sprinkle on pepper. On one side of sandwiches layer cucumber, sprouts, lettuce, turkey bacon and tomato. Cover with remaining toast.

Vegetarian Pita Pockets with Cucumber Yogurt Dressing

> 1 medium zucchini, sliced into thin, 2-inch strips
> 1/2 large red bell pepper, sliced into thin 2-inch strips
> 1/2 medium carrot, sliced into thin 2-inch strips
> 1/8 cabbage head, finely chopped
> 1/2 teaspoon garlic powder
> 4 6-inch pita breads

Dressing
1/2 cup plain low-fat yogurt
1/2 teaspoon dried dill
1/4 cup chopped cucumbers
dash black pepper

In small bowl, stir together dressing ingredients. Set aside.

In casserole dish, place vegetables. Sprinkle with garlic powder. Cover and microwave on HIGH for 4-6 minutes until vegetables are tender crisp, stirring once. Drain.

Wrap pita breads in paper towel and microwave on HIGH for 1 minute until heated through. Slit and fill with vegetables and yogurt dressing.

Toasted Cheese Sandwich with Crinkled Turkey and Cucumber

A nice light brunch.

2 medium tomatoes, sliced crosswise
1 large cucumber, sliced into 1/4-inch-thick rounds
2 English muffins, sliced in half, toasted
1/2 cup shredded low-fat cheddar cheese
1/2 diced jalapeño chili pepper (optional)
1/8 cup diced ripe olives for garnish
8 ounces turkey lunch meat, 8 thin slices

Divide tomato and cucumber slices among 4 serving plates. Place English muffin in toaster. Meanwhile shred cheese and chop jalapeño pepper and olives. Separate turkey slices and arrange, overlapping around edge of microwaveable pie plate. Cover with wax paper and microwave on HIGH for 2-4 minutes until heated through.

Divide turkey onto same serving plates. Sprinkle cheese on English muffin halves, place on paper towel and microwave on HIGH for 1 minute to melt cheese. Garnish with jalapeño pepper and olives and place on bed of crinkled turkey.

Tuna Souffle Sandwiches

8 servings

> 1/2 cup diced green bell pepper
> 1/4 cup diced onion
> 1 (6 1/2-ounce) can white tuna packed in water, drained
> 1 cup liquid egg substitute
> 1/2 teaspoon garlic powder
> 1/2 teaspoon parsley flakes
> 4 English muffins, halved and toasted
> 2 Tablespoons chopped pimiento for garnish
> 2 Tablespoons chopped green onion for garnish

Combine bell pepper and onion in casserole dish. Cover and microwave on HIGH for 1 minute. Add tuna, egg substitute, garlic powder and parsley flakes. Cook on MEDIUM (50% power) for 7-9 minutes until hot throughout, stirring every 2 minutes. Spoon onto hot toasted English muffins and garnish with pimiento and green onions. Serve open faced.

SOUPS

Shrimp Soup with Red Beans and Rice

1 teaspoon vegetable oil
1 cup chopped onion
1/2 cup chopped celery
2 cloves minced garlic
1 cup instant brown rice
1 1/4 cups water
2 cups chicken broth
1 (14 1/2-ounce) can low-sodium crushed tomatoes
1 teaspoon chili powder
1/2 teaspoon cumin
3/4 pound small peeled fresh or frozen shrimp
1 (15 1/2-ounce) can drained red beans
1 Tablespoon lime juice

Combine oil, onion, celery and garlic in casserole dish. Cook on HIGH for 2-3 minutes until onions and celery are tender-crisp.

Add rice, water, broth, tomatoes and spices. Stir well. Cover and cook on HIGH for 12-15 minutes until rice is done.

Stir in shrimp, red beans and lime juice. Cover and cook on HIGH 3-5 minutes until shrimp is done and beans are hot. Let stand 5 minutes.

Hearty Minestrone

1 large chopped onion
2 cloves minced garlic
2 small crookneck squash, sliced
1 stalk celery, sliced
4 cups chicken broth
1 (28-ounce) can low-sodium chopped tomatoes.
1/2 cup instant brown rice
1 (15 1/2-ounce) can white beans
1 (10-ounce) package frozen chopped spinach
1/2 teaspoon dried basil
1/2 teaspoon dried parsley
1/4 teaspoon dried oregano
1/3 cup grated Parmesan cheese

In large casserole dish combine onion, garlic, and squash. Cover and cook on HIGH for 3-4 minutes until vegetables are tender-crisp.

Add remaining ingredients except cheese. Cover and cook on HIGH 10 minutes. Reduce heat to MEDIUM (50% power). Re-cover and cook for 15-20 minutes until heated through and flavors have blended. Pour into serving bowls and top with Parmesan cheese.

Chicken, Vegetables and Rice Soup

Great with fresh baked bread on a rainy night.

> 6 cups low-salt chicken broth
> 1 pound chicken breasts, skin and fat removed
> 3 chopped carrots
> 1 medium chopped onion
> 1 cup frozen peas
> 1/2 cup instant brown rice
> 8 ounces fresh sliced mushrooms
> 1/2 teaspoon garlic powder
> 1 teaspoon parsley flakes
> 1/4 teaspoon pepper

Combine water, broth, chicken, carrots and onion in a 3-quart casserole dish. Cover and cook on HIGH for 15-20 minutes until chicken is tender, stirring twice.

Remove chicken, chop into bite-size pieces and return to soup. Add peas, rice, mushrooms and herbs. Stir, cover, and cook on HIGH for 9-12 minutes until rice is done. Let stand 5 minutes before serving.

Turkey Noodle Soup

1/4 cup white wine
2 sliced carrots
1 small eggplant (1 1/2 cups) peeled and chopped
1 medium chopped onion
8 ounces fresh sliced mushrooms
3 large garlic cloves, minced
6 cups low-salt chicken broth
1 (15-ounce) can stewed cut up tomatoes with their
  juice
2 Tablespoons fresh minced parsley
2 cups diced cooked turkey, fat and skin removed.
1/2 cup thin eggless noodles

Combine wine, carrots, eggplant, onion, mushrooms and garlic in a 3-quart casserole dish. Cover and microwave 8-10 minutes until vegetables are tender, stirring twice. Stir in broth, tomatoes, and parsley. Cover and cook on HIGH 20 to 25 minutes, stirring twice. Add turkey and noodles. Cover and microwave on HIGH for 4-6 minutes until noodles are almost completely soft in the center. Let stand 5 minutes.

Onion Soup

2 medium onions, sliced and separated into rings
1/4 cup diced green onion
1 Tablespoon olive oil
3 cups hot water
1 teaspoon Worcestershire sauce
1 teaspoon beef bouillon granules
1/4 teaspoon black pepper
12 fat-free whole wheat crackers
3 ounces fat-free mozzarella cheese

Combine olive oil and onions in 2-quart casserole dish. Cover and microwave on HIGH for 6-8 minutes until onions are tender, stirring twice. Add water, Worcestershire sauce, bouillon and pepper. Cover and microwave on HIGH 6-8 minutes, or until boiling. Reduce power to MEDIUM (50% power) and cook an additional 6 minutes. Divide soup into 4 individual microwaveable serving bowls. Top each with crackers and cheeses. Microwave on HIGH 1-2 minutes until cheese melts.

Vegetable and Meatball Soup

    1 large onion, chopped
    2 carrots, chopped
    2 stalks celery, chopped
    3 small red potatoes, sliced
    3 cloves garlic, minced
    4 cups low-salt chicken broth
    4 cups low-salt crushed tomatoes in their juice
    1/4 teaspoon basil
    1/4 teaspoon black pepper
    1 cup fresh sliced mushrooms
    1/2 cup small macaroni
    1 pound of meatballs (see recipe on page 161)

Combine onion, carrots, celery, potatoes, garlic and 1/4 cup of the broth in a 3-quart casserole dish. Cover and cook on HIGH for 10-12 minutes until vegetables are tender-crisp. Add broth, tomatoes, basil and pepper, stirring well. Cover and cook on HIGH for 8 minutes. Stir in mushrooms, meatballs, and macaroni. Cover and cook on HIGH for 5-7 minutes until mushrooms and macaroni are done.

Cabbage and Rice Soup

serves 6

    4 slices turkey-bacon, chopped
    1 medium head cabbage, chopped
    1 medium red onion, sliced into rings
    1 1/2 teaspoon chicken bouillon granules
    1/4 teaspoon dill weed
    1/8 teaspoon pepper
    1/4 cup instant brown rice
    5 cups hot water, divided

Place turkey-bacon in 3-quart casserole dish. Cover and microwave on HIGH for 2-3 minutes until turkey-bacon starts crisping. Add cabbage, onion, seasonings and 2 cups of hot water. Cover and microwave on HIGH for 10 minutes. Stir in rice and 3 cups water. Cover and microwave on HIGH for 8-10 minutes until rice is cooked and cabbage is tender.

Split Pea Soup

serves 6

>   4 slices turkey-bacon, chopped
>   1 1/4 cups (8 ounces) dried split peas
>   1 medium onion, finely chopped
>   5 cups chicken broth
>   1/2 teaspoon garlic powder
>   1/4 teaspoon oregano
>   1/4 teaspoon pepper
>   1 bay leaf
>   1 cup thinly sliced carrots
>   3/4 cup chopped celery

In 4-quart casserole dish, arrange turkey bacon. Microwave on
HIGH for 2-3 minutes to desired crispness. Add remainder of
ingredients to turkey bacon. Cover and microwave on HIGH for
15 minutes. Stir, re-cover. Reduce power to MEDIUM LOW (30%
power) and simmer for 50-60 minutes until peas are tender,
stirring occasionally.

Miso Soup with Tofu Cubes

>   4 cups water
>   2 packages. Miso- Cup instant soup mix
>   1 cup firm tofu, cubed
>   3 stalks celery, sliced
>   2 green onions, sliced
>   1/8 teaspoon ground ginger

Pour water into a 2-quart casserole dish. Cover and microwave
on HIGH for 4-5 minutes until boiling. Add soup mix, tofu,
celery, onions and ginger. Stir. Cover and microwave on HIGH
for 5 minutes or until vegetables are tender-crisp.

Hamburger Vegetable Soup

>1/2 pound extra lean ground beef
>1 large potato, peeled and cubed
>1 cup frozen corn
>1 medium zucchini, cut lengthwise then sliced
>1 cup frozen peas
>1 medium onion, chopped
>6 cups salt-free chunky tomatoes with juice, divided
>2 teaspoons basil
>1/4 teaspoon celery salt
>1 teaspoon dill weed
>3/4 cup fresh sliced mushrooms

Place beef in plastic microwaveable colander and place colander in bowl to catch drippings. Microwave on HIGH for 4-6 minutes until meat is no longer pink, stirring twice to break apart meat. Let stand.

In 3-quart casserole dish, combine potato, corn, zucchini, peas, onion and 1/4 cup tomatoes with juice. Cover and cook on HIGH for 10-12 minutes until vegetables are tender. Pour in remainder of tomatoes, seasonings, ground beef and mushrooms. Cover and cook on HIGH for 5-6 minutes then reduce power to MEDIUM LOW (30% power) and simmer for 15 minutes.

New England Clam Chowder

>4 slices turkey-bacon-chopped
>2 large red skinned potatoes, finely chopped
>1 large carrot, finely chopped
>2 Tablespoons water
>1 medium onion, chopped
>2 Tablespoons all-purpose flour
>dash cayenne pepper
>1/4 teaspoon thyme
>3 cups skim milk
>1 (6 1/2-ounce) can minced clams with liquid.

Place bacon in a 3-quart casserole dish. Microwave on HIGH for 2-3 minutes to desired crispness. Remove grease. Set bacon aside.

To same casserole dish, add potatoes, carrot, water and onion. Cover and cook on HIGH for 8-10 minutes, until potatoes are fork-tender, stirring once.

Stir in flour, pepper, thyme, milk and clams with liquid. Cover and cook on HIGH for 4-6 minutes until hot and slightly thickened, stirring after each minute.

Mushroom Soup

> 1 pound fresh mushrooms, sliced
> 1/2 cup chopped green onion
> 3 cups nonfat milk
> 1/2 teaspoon Worcestershire sauce
> 1/8 teaspoon black pepper
> 1/4 teaspoon thyme
> 2 Tablespoons diced parsley

In 2-quart casserole dish, combine mushrooms and green onion. Cover and cook on HIGH for 3 minutes, stirring once. Add milk, Worcestershire sauce, pepper, thyme and parsley. Stir. Cover and cook on HIGH for 4-6 minutes until heated through, stirring once.

Crunchy Oriental Mushroom Soup

> 4 cups hot water
> 3 teaspoons low-salt chicken bouillon granules
> 2 teaspoons low-salt soy sauce
> 1/4 cup chopped green onion
> 1/4 cup chopped celery
> 6 ounces fresh sliced mushrooms
> 1 (8-ounce) can sliced water chestnuts

In 2-quart casserole dish, combine water, seasonings, onion and celery. Cover and microwave on HIGH for 4-5 minutes until celery is tender-crisp, stirring once. Add mushrooms and water chestnuts. Cover and cook on HIGH for 3-5 minutes until mushrooms are soft.

Egg Drop Soup

> 2 cups hot water
> 1 (10 1/2-ounce) can chicken broth
> 3 teaspoons low-salt soy sauce
> 4 Tablespoons chopped green onion
> 4 Tablespoons diced cabbage
> 1/4 cup egg substitute, slightly beaten

In a 2-quart casserole dish, combine water, chicken broth, soy sauce, onion and cabbage. Microwave on HIGH for 8-12 minutes until boiling. Pour egg in a thin stream over broth, let threads set. Serve immediately.

Chilled Carrot and Yam Soup

> 1 clove garlic, minced
> 1 medium onion, chopped
> 1/3 cup orange juice
> 1/2 pound carrots, peeled, cut into 1/2 inch slices
> 1 cup peeled, coarsely chopped yam
> 1/2 cup + 4 teaspoons fat-free plain yogurt
> 2 cups chicken broth
> 1/8 teaspoon nutmeg
> dash cayenne pepper
> 1/8 teaspoon black pepper
> freshly chopped parsley for garnish

In a 2 1/2-quart casserole dish, combine garlic, onion, orange juice, carrots and yam. Cover and cook on HIGH for 6-8 minutes until tender, stirring once.

Pour the yogurt and cooked vegetables into a blender and puree. Return to casserole dish and stir in remaining ingredients except for parsley. Chill for at least 1 hour.

To serve, divide into 4 bowls and garnish each with 1 teaspoon of yogurt and sprinkle on parsley.

Gazpacho with Avocado

2 medium tomatoes, diced
4 cups low-salt tomato juice
1/4 cup diced green onion
3 cups diced peeled cucumber
2 cloves garlic, minced
1 jalapeño pepper, minced
2 Tablespoons apple cider vinegar
1 Tablespoon lime juice
1/2 large ripe avocado, sliced thin

Place all ingredients, except avocado, in a 2-quart bowl. Mix well and refrigerate for 1 hour. Before serving, garnish with avocado.

Cauliflower Soup
serves 6

1 Tablespoon olive oil
1 medium onion, chopped
1 clove garlic, minced
1 large cauliflower, cored and chopped
1 teaspoon basil
1 Tablespoon chicken bouillon granules
1/2 teaspoon dried thyme
1/2 teaspoon curry powder
1/8 teaspoon black pepper
1/8 teaspoon ground nutmeg
4 cups water

Combine oil, onion, garlic and cauliflower in a large casserole dish. Cover and cook on HIGH for 8-12 minutes until vegetables are tender. Puree vegetables in a blender. Return to casserole dish, add seasonings and water. Stir well. Cover and microwave on HIGH for 4-6 minutes, stirring twice.

Curried Pumpkin Soup

>1 teaspoon olive oil
>1 cup chopped onion
>1/2 cup diced celery
>1 clove minced garlic
>1 (16-ounce) can pumpkin
>3 cups chicken broth
>2 teaspoons curry powder
>1/4 teaspoon lemon-pepper seasoning
>1 Tablespoon finely chopped green onion for garnish

Place oil, onion, celery and garlic in 3-quart casserole dish. Cover and microwave on HIGH for 3-4 minutes until vegetables are tender, stirring once.

Blend in remaining ingredients except green onions. Microwave on HIGH for 6-9 minutes until hot through, stirring twice. Top with green onions.

Cream of Potato Soup

serves 8

>4 slices turkey-bacon
>2 large potatoes, peeled and diced
>2 cups chopped celery
>1 medium onion, chopped
>2 teaspoons olive oil
>2 Tablespoons all purpose flour
>2 cups boiling water
>3 cups nonfat milk
>3 teaspoons chicken bouillon granules
>1/4 teaspoon celery seed
>1/4 teaspoon black pepper

Place turkey-bacon on double layer of paper towel in oven and cover with another paper towel. Microwave on HIGH for 2-3 minutes to desired crispness. Chop.

In 3-quart casserole dish, combine turkey bacon, potatoes, celery, onion, oil, and 1/2 cup of the water. Cover and microwave on HIGH for 10-15 minutes until vegetables are tender, stirring twice.

49

Add flour, stir. Add the rest of the water, milk, and seasonings, stirring well. Cover with wax paper and microwave on HIGH for 7-9 minutes until hot, but not boiling, stirring twice.

Chinese Broth Soup with Celery and Tofu

> 2 cups hot water
> 1 (10 1/2-ounce) can chicken broth
> 3 teaspoons low-salt soy sauce
> 2 cups celery, sliced
> 1 cup cubed tofu
> 1/4 teaspoon black pepper

Combine water, chicken broth, soy sauce, and celery in 2-quart casserole dish. Microwave on HIGH for 7-12 minutes until celery is tender. Add tofu and pepper and let stand 5 minutes.

Chard and Broken Vermicelli in Chicken Broth

> 1 medium onion, sliced, rings separated
> 1 Tablespoon olive oil
> 2 Tablespoons water
> 1 bunch (approx. 4 cups) coarsely chopped chard
> 6 cups chicken broth
> 4 ounces vermicelli, broken into 1/2 inch lengths
> salt-free seasoning
> black pepper to taste

Place onion, water and olive oil in a 3-quart casserole dish. Cover and microwave on HIGH for 3-4 minutes until onion is soft.

Add chard and chicken broth. Cover and cook on HIGH for 5 minutes. Reduce heat to MEDIUM LOW (30% power) and simmer for 10-15 minutes.

Add vermicelli and seasonings. Cover and microwave on HIGH for 3-4 minutes until vermicelli is cooked al dente.

Celery Mushroom Soup

3 cups low-salt chicken broth, divided
1 pound celery stalks, trimmed and cut into 1-inch
   pieces
1 large onion, chopped coarsely
4 medium mushrooms, sliced
dash black pepper

In a 3-quart casserole dish, combine 1 cup broth with celery and onion. Cover and microwave on HIGH for 10 minutes.

Puree mixture with a blender or food processor and return to casserole dish. Add remaining broth, mushrooms and pepper and microwave, covered, on HIGH for 3 minutes until hot.

Small Shell Pasta with Broth and Tomatoes

1 teaspoon olive oil
1 large clove garlic, crushed
1/4 cup chopped onion
1 (15-ounce) can low-salt stewed tomatoes
1 (15-ounce) can low-fat chicken broth
1/3 cup frozen peas
1 cup small shell pasta

In a 2 1/2-quart casserole dish, combine oil, garlic and onion. Cover and cook on HIGH for 2 minutes. Pour in remainder of ingredients except for pasta shells. Cover and cook on HIGH for 7 minutes. Add shells. Cover and cook on MEDIUM (50% power) for 10 minutes until pasta is cooked.

Easy Creamed Corn Soup

> 1 small onion, chopped
> 2 (15-ounce) cans cream style corn
> 2 cups nonfat milk
> 1/4 teaspoon black pepper

In a 2 1/2-quart casserole dish, cook onion on HIGH for 2 minutes until tender. Stir in corn, milk and pepper. Cover and microwave on HIGH for 10 minutes until heated through, stirring twice.

SALADS

Taco Salad

1/2 pound ground turkey
1 cup cooked kidney beans
1 medium onion, diced
1/3 cup low-salt lite ketchup
1 teaspoon chili powder
1/2 teaspoon ground cumin
dash black pepper
dash paprika
6 cups shredded lettuce
2 large tomatoes, chopped
2 green onions, chopped
8 chopped black olives

Combine ground turkey and onion in microwaveable plastic colander. Set colander in bowl. Microwave on HIGH 3-4 minutes, until meat is no longer pink, stirring twice to break apart chunks. Place meat mixture in casserole dish, add kidney beans, ketchup, chili powder, cumin, black and red pepper. Stir well. Cover and microwave on HIGH for 2-2 1/2 minutes until beans are hot. Arrange lettuce on 4 plates. In center of each, place 1/4 turkey mixture and 1/4 of tomatoes. Garnish with green onion and olives.

Warm Zucchini and Olive Salad on a Bed of Lettuce

2 Tablespoons olive oil
1 medium onion, thinly sliced, rings separated
1 clove garlic, minced
2 medium tomatoes, chopped
1 large green pepper, chopped
2 medium zucchini, quartered lengthwise and sliced
2 teaspoons red wine vinegar
1 teaspoon sugar
1/2 teaspoon dried oregano
dash black pepper
2 teaspoons capers, rinsed and drained (optional)
1/2 cup pitted Greek or ripe olives, drained, halved
8-12 large lettuce leaves

In a 2-quart casserole dish, combine oil, onion and garlic. Cover and microwave on HIGH for 2-3 minutes until tender-crisp.

Stir in remaining ingredients except for capers, olives and lettuce. Re-cover and cook on HIGH for 10-14 minutes until vegetables are tender, stirring twice.

Stir in capers and olives. Let stand 1 hour at room temperature to allow flavors to develop.

To serve, line 4 salad plates with lettuce leaves and serve vegetable mixture on top.

Black Bean Salad

A salad with a nice balance of flavors and textures.

2 cups cooked black beans
1/2 cup finely chopped red bell pepper
2/3 cup chopped celery
1/3 cup chopped onions
1 Tablespoon lemon juice
1 Tablespoon olive oil

Toss all ingredients together in a medium bowl. Allow to stand for 1 hour to blend flavors.

Colorful Warm Corn Salad

1 Tablespoon olive oil
1 medium onion, chopped
1 clove garlic, minced
2 cups fresh or frozen corn kernels
1 diced red bell pepper
1 medium zucchini, diced
1 teaspoons red wine vinegar
1/4 teaspoon dried basil
1/8 teaspoon black pepper
4 cups mixed salad greens

In a 2 1/2-quart casserole dish, combine oil, onion, garlic, corn bell pepper and zucchini. Cover and microwave on HIGH for 4-5 minutes until tender-crisp, stirring once. Stir in remaining ingredients except for salad greens. Toss well and let stand, covered, for one hour. Line 4 salad plates with greens and spoon corn mixture onto each.

Hot Turkey, New Potato, and Zucchini Salad

>1/4 cup water
>2 medium zucchini, sliced.
>4 red-skinned potatoes, sliced to same size as zucchini slices
>2 cups cooked turkey, chopped into bite-sized bits
>1/4 cup ripe olives, chopped
>1/2 cup plain low-fat yogurt
>1/4 cup low-fat mayonnaise or mayonnaise substitute
>1/4 teaspoon black pepper
>1/2 teaspoon dry mustard
>1/2 teaspoon celery seed
>1 Tablespoon dried parsley
>1/4 teaspoon paprika

In a 2-quart casserole dish, place water, zucchini and potatoes. Cover and microwave on HIGH for 10-12 minutes until tender. Drain. In a large bowl, stir together olives, yogurt, mayonnaise and seasonings. Stir in turkey. Gently mix in potatoes and zucchini. Top with a sprinkle of paprika.

Warm Crab Meat Pasta Salad on Spinach Bed

>4 cups cooked spiral pasta
>2 cups imitation crab meat picked into small pieces
>2 teaspoons lemon juice
>1/2 teaspoon dried dill weed
>1/4 cup low-calorie creamy cucumber dressing
>1 large cucumber
>Peeled and finely chopped fresh spinach leaves, rinsed

Combine cooked pasta, crab meat, lemon juice, dill weed and cucumber dressing in a 2 1/2-quart casserole dish. Cover and cook on MEDIUM (50% power) for 6-8 minutes to heat through, stirring twice.

Line 4 salad plates with spinach leaves. Layer on cucumbers and top with warm crab meat pasta mixture.

Green Salad with Oranges and Walnuts and Warm Honey Vinaigrette

4 cups romaine lettuce, washed and dried
1 (16-ounce) can Mandarin orange segments, drained
1/2 cup coarsely chopped walnuts

Dressing
1/3 cup walnut oil
2 Tablespoons red wine vinegar
2 Tablespoons honey
1/2 Tablespoons Dijon-style mustard
1/8 teaspoon black pepper

Combine lettuce, oranges and nuts in a large bowl. In a small bowl, place oil, vinegar, honey, mustard and pepper. Microwave on HIGH for 1-1 1/2 minutes until honey is thin and dressing is warm but not boiling. Stir well. Pour over salad and toss well.

Jicama and Guacamole Salad

Jicama adds a mild, juicy crunch to this salad.

> **2 ripe avocados**
> **1 medium cucumber, chopped**
> **3 Tablespoons lime juice**
> **1 1/2 Tablespoons minced onion**
> **1/8 teaspoon black pepper**
> **1 small bunch red-leaf lettuce, washed, dried and torn**
> **4-6 cups jicama, peeled and cut into 1/2 x 3-inch strips**

Just before serving, mash avocados in a medium bowl. Stir in cucumber, lime juice, onion and pepper. Line 4 salad plates with lettuce, spoon 1/4 of the guacamole onto each, and place jicama strips on the side.

Rice, Green Bean, and Olive Mediterranean Salad

> **3 cups cooked rice**
> **3 cups trimmed green beans, cut into 1 1/2-inch pieces**
> **1 Tablespoon olive oil**
> **1/2 teaspoon dried basil**
> **1/2 teaspoon dried oregano**
> **4 cups lettuce, torn**
> **2 cups spinach, trimmed**
> **1/2 cup olives**
>
> **Dressing**
> **1/3 cup extra-virgin olive oil**
> **2 Tablespoons lemon juice**
> **1 small clove garlic minced**
> **1/2 teaspoon honey**
> **1/2 teaspoon Dijon-style mustard**
> **1 teaspoon salt-free seasoning**

Prepare rice on conventional stove top according to package directions. Meanwhile, combine green beans, oil, basil and oregano in a 2-quart casserole dish. Cover and microwave on HIGH for 5-8 minutes until green beans are fork-tender.

In a large bowl, combine lettuce, spinach and olives with dressing. Add rice and green beans and toss well.

Oil Packed Sun Dried Tomatoes

yields 1/4 cup

> 4 plum tomatoes, sliced in half lengthwise
> dash cayenne pepper
> 1/8 teaspoon garlic salt
> 1/4 cup olive oil

Arrange tomatoes on plate, edges not touching, covered with a paper towel. Microwave on MEDIUM LOW (30% power) for 15 minutes. Rotate plate 1/2 turn and continue to microwave another 15 minutes. Rotate plate 1/4 turn and cook an additional 10-15 minutes until tomatoes are dried but not burnt.. Sprinkle with cayenne pepper and salt.

Place in a small container and cover with oil. Let stand 8 hours.

Warm Sun Dried Tomato Salad

> 6 cups torn lettuce leaves (Bibb, red leaf, romaine)
> 1/4 cup sliced oil packed sun-dried tomatoes, drained
> 1/4 cup chopped walnuts
>
> Dressing
> 3 Tablespoons extra-virgin olive oil
> 1 Tablespoon lemon juice
> 1 small clove garlic, minced
> 1 teaspoon salt-free seasoning
> dash black pepper

In a salad bowl whisk together dressing ingredients. Add lettuce, tomatoes and nuts and toss well.

Make Ahead Crunchy Chicken Salad

 2 1/2 cups cooked chicken, cubed
 1/3 head of cabbage, shredded
 1/3 cup green onions, chopped
 1 (3-ounce) can chow mein noodles
 1 (8-ounce) can water chestnuts
 1/2 cup chopped red bell pepper

 Dressing
 1/4 cup canola oil
 2 Tablespoons rice wine vinegar
 1 Tablespoon honey
 2 Tablespoons low-salt soy sauce
 1/4 teaspoon black pepper

In a small bowl combine dressing ingredients. Mix together salad ingredients in a large bowl. Pour dressing onto salad and toss. Let stand overnight.

Coleslaw

 2 cups green cabbage, shredded
 2 cups red cabbage, shredded
 1 small onion, finely chopped
 2 Tablespoons low-fat mayonnaise or mayonnaise
   substitute
 1 teaspoon salt-free seasoning

Combine all ingredients in a medium bowl, mixing well. Allow to stand for 30 minutes before serving.

Green Bean and Bacon Potato Salad

 1/4 cup water
 1/2 pound green beans, chopped into 1-inch pieces
 8 small new potatoes, chopped into 1/2-inch cubes
 1 Tablespoon olive oil
 1/4 teaspoon black pepper
 1/2 teaspoon garlic powder
 4 slices turkey bacon, chopped
 1/4 cup chopped onion
 1 Tablespoon lemon juice
 2 Tablespoons white wine
 2 teaspoons sugar

Place water, green beans and potatoes in baking dish. Cover and cook on HIGH for 5-8 minutes until vegetables are tender. Sprinkle with olive oil, pepper and garlic powder. Let stand.

In a 1 1/2-quart casserole dish, place turkey bacon and onions. Cover and cook on HIGH for 2-3 minutes. Stir in lemon juice, sugar and wine. Cover and microwave on HIGH for 2-3 minutes, stirring once. Pour bacon mixture over potatoes and green beans and toss.

Hot Tuna and Pasta Salad

> 2 cups cooked miniature shells or other small pasta
> 2 medium tomatoes, chopped
> 1/2 cup celery, chopped
> 2 (6 1/2-ounce) cans tuna packed in water, drained
> 8 black ripe olives, sliced
> 1/4 cup low-fat herb vinaigrette dressing
> 1/4 cup (2 ounces) crumbled feta cheese

Prepare pasta according to package directions on conventional stove top. In a 2-quart casserole dish combine tomatoes, celery, tuna, olives, vinaigrette dressing and cooked pasta. Mix well. Cover, and microwave on MEDIUM (50% power) for 4 minutes to warm, stirring once. Garnish with feta cheese.

Cajun Shrimp Salad

> 1 1/2 cups instant brown rice
> 1 1/4 cups water
> 1/4 cup celery, chopped
> 1/4 chopped onion
> 1 small clove garlic, minced
> 1 (16-ounce) can low-salt chopped tomatoes
> 2 Tablespoons tomato paste
> 1 green bell pepper, seeded and chopped
> 1 teaspoon Worcestershire sauce
> 1/4 teaspoon cayenne pepper
> 1/2 teaspoon chili powder
> 2 cups shelled, de-veined shrimp
> 4 cups shredded lettuce

Combine water and rice in 2-quart bowl. Cover and microwave on HIGH for 8 minutes. Let stand.

In a 2-quart casserole dish, combine celery, onion, garlic, tomatoes, tomato paste, bell pepper and seasonings. Cover and cook on HIGH for 4-6 minutes until vegetables are tender-crisp, stirring twice. Stir in shrimp, cover and cook on HIGH an additional 3-4 minutes.

Spoon rice over a bed of lettuce on individual serving plates. Spoon shrimp sauce over rice.

Midwestern Potato Salad

> 3 cups peeled potatoes cut into 1/2-inch cubes (about 4 medium potatoes)
> 1 cup carrots, cut into 1/2-inch cubes
> 1/4 cup water
> 1 cup chopped celery
> 1/4 cup chopped onion
> 1/4 cup fat-free mayonnaise or mayonnaise substitute
> 1 teaspoon vinegar
> dash salt
> 1/4 teaspoon black pepper
> 1/2 teaspoon honey
> 1 green onion, chopped, to garnish
> 6 pitted olives for garnish

Place potatoes, carrots and water in 3-quart casserole. Cover and cook on HIGH for 5-7 minutes until fork-tender, stirring once. Drain in colander.

Combine celery, onion, mayonnaise, vinegar, salt, pepper and honey in large bowl. Stir in potatoes, being careful not to smash them. Garnish with green onion and olives.

Sweet Bacon and Broccoli Salad

4 slices turkey-bacon, chopped
1 large bunch fresh broccoli, top chopped into 1/2-inch size pieces
1/4 cup thinly sliced red onion
1/2 cup coarsely chopped pecans
1/2 cup golden raisins

Dressing
1/4 cup low-fat mayonnaise or mayonnaise substitute
1/3 cup plain fat-free yogurt
2 Tablespoons honey
1 teaspoon vinegar

Stir together dressing ingredients in a small bowl. Set aside.

Arrange bacon on microwaveable plate. Cover with paper towel. Microwave on HIGH for 2-3 minutes to desired crispness.

In a large bowl, toss together, bacon, broccoli, onion, pecans, raisins and dressing.

Kidney Bean and Potato Salad

3 medium red potatoes, cut in 1/2-inch cubes
1/2 cup hot water
2 cups cooked kidney beans
1/2 cup chopped celery
1/4 cup chopped onions
1/2 teaspoon garlic powder
1/8 teaspoon black pepper
3 Tablespoons reduced calorie mayonnaise or mayonnaise substitute

In a 2-quart casserole, place potatoes and hot water. Cover and microwave on HIGH for 4-7 minutes until potatoes are fork-tender. Drain.

Add beans, celery, seasonings and mayonnaise to potatoes. Mix carefully to avoid mashing potatoes and beans.

Warm Sliced Tomato Salad with Parmesan

> 4 medium firm ripe tomatoes, sliced crosswise
> 2 Tablespoons olive oil
> 1 Tablespoon grated Parmesan cheese
> 1/4 teaspoon garlic salt
> 1/8 teaspoon black pepper

Arrange tomato slices in an overlapping circle on a microwaveable serving platter. Drizzle with oil, sprinkle with cheese, salt, and pepper. Cover with wax paper. Microwave on HIGH for 1 1/2-3 minutes until just heated through.

Winter Salad with Pecan Coated Mozzarella

> 4 ounces low-fat Mozzarella cheese cut into 4 1/2-inch thick slices
> 1 Tablespoon olive oil
> 1/4 cup finely chopped pecans
> 1 small head red-leaf lettuce, washed and dried
> 1 small bunch spinach, stems removed, washed and dried
> 1 small red onion, thinly sliced, rings separated
> 1 red apple, unpeeled, cored, sliced for garnish

> Dressing
> 2 Tablespoons extra-virgin olive oil
> 2 teaspoons lemon juice
> 1/2 teaspoon Dijon-style mustard
> 1/4 teaspoon garlic powder
> salt and pepper to taste

Pour oil in shallow bowl. Place the pecans in another shallow bowl. Dip both sides of each cheese slice first in the oil then the nuts. Place coated cheese on a microwaveable plate, edges not touching.

Whisk the dressing ingredients together in the bottom of a large salad bowl. Add the greens and onion and toss.

Divide salad among 4 salad bowls and garnish with apple slices. Place uncovered plate with cheese in oven and microwave on MEDIUM (50% power) for 1-2 minutes until warm to the touch. With a spatula, top each salad with the cheese.

Mediterranean Chicken Salad

> 1 1/2 cups cooked chicken or turkey, diced
> 1/2 cup red bell pepper, chopped
> 1/2 cup black or green olives, sliced
> 1 (6-ounce) jar artichoke hearts, drained and chopped
> 1/8 cup red onion, diced
> 1/4 cup low-calorie mayonnaise or mayonnaise substitute
> 1 Tablespoon red wine vinegar
> 1/2 teaspoon dried oregano, crumbled
> 1 clove garlic, minced
> pepper

In a medium bowl, mix together chicken, red pepper, olives, artichoke hearts and onions. In small bowl, whisk mayonnaise, vinegar, garlic and oregano. Add mayonnaise mixture to chicken mixture and stir well. Season to taste with pepper. Cover and microwave on MEDIUM (50% power) for 3-4 minutes to warm, stirring once.

Serve on a bed of lettuce or in a small loaf of French bread.

Red Pepper and Mushroom Salad

> 1 medium red bell pepper, sliced into 1/4 x 2-inch strips
> 1/2 pound fresh mushrooms, sliced
> 1 Tablespoon olive oil
> 1 teaspoon lemon juice
> 1/4 teaspoon garlic salt
> 1/8 teaspoon black pepper
> 1/8 teaspoon dried oregano
> 1/2 teaspoon dried basil

Mix mushrooms and bell pepper in serving bowl. In small bowl, whisk together remaining ingredients. Just before serving, pour dressing on vegetables and mix lightly.

Marinated Green Beans and Mushrooms with Almonds

1 pound green beans, trimmed and cut into 1 1/2-inch
    pieces
12 ounces medium mushrooms, quartered
1/4 cup sliced almonds
8 large lettuce leaves

Marinade
3 Tablespoons olive oil
1 Tablespoon red wine vinegar
1 teaspoon Dijon-style mustard

In a 2-quart casserole dish, combine marinade ingredients. Add mushrooms and microwave on HIGH for 2 minutes stirring once. Reserve marinade and remove mushrooms with slotted spoon, placing in a bowl.

Place green beans into same dish with marinade. Cover and cook on HIGH for 3-5 minutes until tender crisp, stirring once. Stir mushrooms back into marinade with beans, cover and refrigerate for 1 hour.

To serve, line serving plate with lettuce and spoon green bean-mushroom mixture on top. Sprinkle with almonds and drizzle with remaining marinade.

Turkey Apple Salad

3 cups cooked turkey, diced
2 medium apples, diced
1/2 cup sunflower seeds
3 Tablespoons finely chopped fresh parsley
1/3-1/2 cup low-fat cucumber salad dressing
1 small bunch red-leaf lettuce

In a medium-sized bowl, stir together turkey, apple, sunflower seeds and parsley. Pour dressing over turkey mixture and toss. Serve over bed of lettuce leaves.

Fresh Spinach and Smoked Salmon Salad

>1 pound spinach, washed, trimmed and torn
>3 Tablespoons olive oil
>2 Tablespoons fresh lemon juice
>1 teaspoon salt-free seasoning
>1/3 pound thinly sliced smoked salmon
>1/2 teaspoon dried dill weed, for garnish

Place spinach in a salad bowl. Whisk oil, lemon juice and seasoning in a small bowl, microwave on HIGH for 2 minutes until warm. Pour over spinach and toss. Divide spinach among 4 salad plates, top with the smoked salmon and sprinkle with dill.

Tuna and Black Eyed Peas Salad

>1 (6 1/2-ounce) can white tuna, packed in water,
>   drained
>1/2 cup plain low-fat yogurt
>3 Tablespoons finely chopped onion
>8 ripe olives, chopped
>1 cup cooked black eyed peas
>1/4 teaspoon chili powder
>salad greens

In a medium bowl, combine tuna, yogurt, onion, olives, black eyed peas, and chili powder. Microwave on MEDIUM (50% power) for 3-4 minutes to heat through. To serve, line plates with salad greens and spoon tuna-black eyed pea mixture on top.

Mushroom and Artichoke Stuffed Tomatoes

>4 medium tomatoes
>1 (6-ounce) jar artichoke hearts, drained and chopped
>2 cups fresh mushrooms, coarsely chopped
>1/4 cup chopped onions
>1/4 cup Italian-style bread crumbs
>1/4 cup shredded low-fat Cheddar cheese

Starting at the top of the tomato, in the stem area, cut to form 6 wedges, being careful not to cut completely through the bottom. Open to form a star formation.

In a medium bowl, combine artichoke hearts, mushrooms and onion. Cover and microwave on HIGH for 5 minutes until vegetables are tender. Stir in bread crumbs.

Arrange tomatoes on serving plates, spoon mushroom mixture on top, and sprinkle with cheese.

Whole Wheat Croutons

Avoid the unwholesome ingredients of commercial croutons.

4 slices whole wheat bread (average size) crusts removed and sliced into 1/2-inch cubes

Line bottom of oven with a double layer of paper towel. Place bread cubes on top in an even layer. Microwave uncovered on HIGH for 2-3 minutes until dried.

Basil-Garlic Croutons

1/4-1/3 loaf French bread, sliced 1/2-inch thick and cut into 2-inch pieces
1/4 cup olive oil
2 cloves garlic, finely minced
1/2 teaspoon dried basil

Line the bottom of a large baking dish with paper towel. Place bread on the towel. Microwave on HIGH for 2-3 minutes, until bread is just dried but not brown. Set aside.

Combine oil and garlic in a bowl. Cook on HIGH for 1 minute. Remove paper towel from dish and rearrange bread. Brush oil mixture onto bread and sprinkle with basil. Microwave on HIGH for 1-2 minutes until croutons are crisp.

VEGETABLES

Baked Russet Potatoes

4 Russet potatoes (6-8 ounces each)

Wash potatoes and pierce in several places. Arrange potatoes in microwave oven so that they are not touching. Cook on HIGH for 10-12 minutes until almost tender in centers, turning and rearranging once. Wrap in foil or cover with an inverted bowl, and let stand 5 minutes.

Squash and Mushroom Stuffing

yields 2 cups

2 Tablespoons water
1/2 cup chopped mushrooms
1/2 cup cubed squash
1/2 cup chopped celery
1/2 cup chopped onion
1/4 cup drained, sun-dried tomatoes, oil pack
1 cup seasoned croutons
1 teaspoon low-salt chicken bouillon granules
1 teaspoon dried sage
1 teaspoon dried thyme

In a 2 1/2-quart casserole dish, combine water, mushrooms, squash, celery, onion and tomato. Cover and microwave on HIGH for 6-7 minutes until tender. Drain. Stir in croutons, bouillon granules, sage and thyme. Use as a stuffing for poultry or as a side dish.

Zucchini Strips with Sesame Seeds

1 large (about 1/2 pound) zucchini, cut into 1/4 x 2-inch strips
2 medium (about 1/2 pound) crookneck squash, cut into 1/4 x 2-inch strips
3 Tablespoons minced onion

1 Tablespoon sesame seeds
1 teaspoon fresh chopped basil or 1/2 teaspoon dried
   basil
1 teaspoon sesame oil
dash white pepper

In a 2-quart casserole dish, place zucchini and crookneck squash.
Sprinkle with onion, sesame seeds, basil, oil and white pepper.
Cover and microwave on HIGH for 5-7 minutes until vegetables
are tender, stirring once.

Steamed Green Beans

1/4 cup water
1 1/2 pounds fresh green beans, trimmed
1 medium onion, sliced into rings
1 teaspoon lemon-pepper seasoning

In a 2-quart casserole dish, place water, beans and onions. Cover
and cook on HIGH for 10-12 minutes until vegetables are tender.
Drain and sprinkle with lemon-pepper seasoning.

Squash Stuffed Potatoes

1 pound butternut squash
2 large baking potatoes
2 Tablespoons margarine
1/8 cup skim milk
1/4 teaspoon cumin
1 teaspoon salt-free seasoning
dash black pepper
dash paprika

Pierce squash in several places with a fork. Place on a paper
towel in oven and microwave on HIGH for 6-8 minutes until
soft. Let stand 20 minutes to cool.

Pierce potatoes in several places with a fork. Wrap in paper
towel and microwave on HIGH for 8-10 minutes until soft.

71

Slice potatoes in half lengthwise and spoon cooked potato into a medium bowl, taking care not to break skins, Cut squash in half, discard center strings and seeds, and spoon cooked halves into bowl with potatoes.

Add margarine, skim milk, cumin and salt-free seasoning to potatoes and squash. Mash. Spoon back into potato skins. Sprinkle with pepper and paprika and reheat in microwave on HIGH for 2-3 minutes until heated through.

Pureed Carrots with Pine Nuts or Almonds

6 medium carrots, sliced
1 cup water
1 teaspoon chicken bouillon granules
1 teaspoon honey
3 Tablespoons minced green onion
3 Tablespoons whole pine nuts or slivered almonds

In a 2-quart casserole dish combine all ingredients except green onion and nuts. Cover and microwave on HIGH for 6-8 minutes until carrots are soft, stirring every 3 minutes.

Place carrots with liquid in a blender and puree. Stir in green onion. Place in a serving dish and garnish with pine nuts or almonds.

Snow Peas and Bean Sprouts

6 ounces fresh snow peas, trimmed
1 pound bean sprouts
1 cup fresh mushrooms, sliced
1 teaspoon sesame oil
1 Tablespoon lite soy sauce

Combine all ingredients in a 1 1/2-quart casserole dish. Cover and cook on HIGH for 3-4 minutes until peas are tender-crisp.

Mashed Potatoes with Cabbage

2 medium potatoes, peeled and cubed
2 Tablespoons water
2 cups shredded cabbage
1/4 cup skimmed milk
2 Tablespoons margarine
1 teaspoon onion powder
1 teaspoon salt-free seasoning
1/8 teaspoon black pepper
dash paprika for garnish

In a 2-quart casserole dish combine water and potatoes. Cover and cook on HIGH for 6-7 minutes until fork-soft, stirring once. Let stand 5 minutes.

Meanwhile, put shredded cabbage in a 2-quart casserole dish, cover, and microwave on HIGH for 4-6 minutes until tender. Set aside.

Mash potatoes with milk, margarine, onion powder, seasoning and pepper. Stir in shredded cabbage. Serve.

Vegetables Romano

3 cups celery, diagonally sliced
1/2 medium red bell pepper, chopped
3/4 cup fresh sliced mushrooms
1/4 cup fresh parsley, chopped
1 teaspoon olive oil
2 Tablespoons grated Romano cheese
dash black pepper

In a 2 1/2-quart casserole dish, combine all ingredients except cheese and black pepper. Cover and microwave on HIGH for 6-7 minutes until celery is tender, stirring twice during cooking time. Drain. Sprinkle with cheese and black pepper.

Spaghetti Squash with Sauce

> 1 large (4 pound) spaghetti squash, pierced with knife
>   in several places
> 1 (26-ounce) chunky old-fashioned spaghetti sauce.
> 4 large fresh mushrooms, chopped, for garnish
> 2 Tablespoons grated Parmesan cheese, for garnish

Place squash on a paper towel in oven and microwave on HIGH for 12 minutes, rotating and turning each 4 minutes to ensure even cooking. Let stand 10 minutes.

Pour spaghetti sauce into a medium bowl and heat on HIGH for 3-4 minutes until heated through. Slit squash lengthwise and remove seeds. Using a fork, rake out spaghetti strands. Pour hot spaghetti sauce over squash and garnish with mushrooms and cheese.

Sautéed Mushrooms and Onions

> 1 large onion, sliced into rings
> 1 1/2 cups sliced fresh mushrooms
> 3 Tablespoons white wine
> 1 teaspoon beef bouillon granules
> 1/4 teaspoon dry mustard
> 1/2 teaspoon dry basil
> 1/8 teaspoon black pepper
> 1/4 teaspoon garlic powder
> 1 small tomato, cut into 8 wedges

In a 2-quart casserole dish, combine onion rings, mushrooms, water, wine and seasonings. Mix well. Cover and microwave on HIGH for 6 minutes until onions are tender, stirring after half the cooking time. Stir in tomato and microwave another 1 minute on HIGH.

Herbed Brussels Sprouts and Carrots

> 2 large carrots, scraped and cut into 1/2 x 2-inch strips
> 10 ounces Brussels sprouts, cut in half
> 1/4 cup water
> 1 teaspoon salt-free seasoning
> 1 Tablespoon margarine

In a 2-quart casserole dish, toss together carrots and Brussels sprouts. Add water. Cover and cook on HIGH for 10-12 minutes until carrots are just tender. Drain. Dot with margarine and toss to coat vegetables.

Squash with Raisins and Walnuts

> 2 Table Queen or Kobacha squash, halved, seeds and
>   membranes removed
> 2 cups water
> 1/4 cup raisins
> 3/4 cup chopped walnuts
> 1/4 cup chopped celery
> 2 Tablespoons maple syrup
> 2 teaspoons margarine

Trim 1/4-inch from rounded outer side of each squash half so they stand level. Place hollow side down in a 9 x 12-inch baking dish and add water. Cover and microwave on HIGH for 10-12 minutes, until almost cooked through. Combine raisins, nuts, celery, syrup and margarine in a small bowl. Drain water from squash, turn squash over, and spoon in filling evenly. Cover and microwave on HIGH for 2-4 minutes until heated through.

Peas and Pearl Onions

> 2 1/2 cups frozen peas
> 2 Tablespoons water
> 1 (5-ounce) can pearl onions
> 2 teaspoons margarine
> 1/2 teaspoon garlic salt
> 1/8 teaspoon black pepper

Pour peas into water in a 1 1/2-quart casserole dish. Cover and microwave on HIGH for 6 minutes, stirring after half the time. Drain. Add onions, margarine, and seasonings.

Cover and microwave on HIGH for 1-3 minutes until peas are tender and heated through.

Eggplant Roma

> 1 medium eggplant (1 pound), cut into 1/2-inch thick slices
> 1/2 medium green bell pepper, diced
> 1 green onion diced
> 1 (15-ounce) can low-salt tomato sauce
> 2 cloves garlic, minced
> 1/4 teaspoon dried oregano
> 1/4 cup shredded low-fat Mozzarella cheese

Arrange eggplant slices in an even layer in a baking dish. Combine remaining ingredients, except for cheese, in a medium bowl. Pour over eggplant. Cover and microwave on HIGH for 8-10 minutes until egg plant is tender. Sprinkle with cheese and let stand 2 minutes, covered to melt cheese.

Lemon Sesame Seed Brussels Sprouts

2 teaspoons sesame seeds
1 pound fresh Brussels sprouts, cut in half
2 Tablespoons water
2 teaspoons lemon juice
2 teaspoons margarine

In a microwaveable cup, microwave sesame seeds on HIGH for 2 1/2-3 minutes or until golden brown. Set aside.

Place Brussels sprouts and water in a 2-quart casserole dish. Cover and cook on HIGH for 6-7 minutes until tender, rearranging vegetables after half the cooking time. Drain. Let stand, covered, 5 minutes.

In a 1-cup measure combine lemon juice and margarine. Microwave on HIGH for 45 seconds. Pour over Brussels sprouts and sprinkle with sesame seeds.

Artichokes with Avocado Dip

A delicious alternative to dipping in butter.

4 medium artichokes
1 cup water, divided
1 large avocado, mashed just before serving
1 Tablespoon lime juice
1/2 teaspoon salt-free seasoning

Trim artichokes and place stem side up with 1/2 cup water in baking dish. Cover with plastic wrap. Microwave on HIGH for 9-10 minutes, until center leaf pulls out easily, rearranging artichokes after half the cooking time. Drain and let stand, covered.

In small bowl, combine remaining ingredients and serve with artichokes.

Green Beans with Almond Sauce

   1 (9-ounce) package frozen cut green beans
   2 teaspoons olive oil
   1 Tablespoon minced onion
   1/4 teaspoon dried basil
   2 Tablespoons finely chopped almonds
   dash pepper

Place green beans in a microwaveable serving bowl. Cover and microwave on HIGH for 6 minutes, stirring after 3 minutes

In a 1-cup measure, combine margarine, onion, and basil. Microwave on HIGH for 1-1 1/2 minutes until onion is soft. Add nuts and stir. Pour over beans and toss. Sprinkle with pepper.

Ratatouille

   8 ounces fresh sliced mushrooms
   1 bell pepper, chopped
   1 Tablespoon olive oil
   2 medium zucchini, cut into 1/2-inch cubes
   1 (16-ounce) can whole tomatoes, drained and coarsely
      chopped
   1 cup finely chopped onions
   2 cloves minced garlic
   2 Tablespoons tomato paste
   2 teaspoons dried basil leaves
   dash black pepper
   3 Tablespoons fresh chopped parsley
   1/4 cup grated Romano cheese

Combine all ingredients except parsley and cheese in a baking dish. Toss well to coat, and arrange evenly. Cover and microwave on HIGH for 10-15 minutes, until vegetables are tender, stirring twice. Stir in parsley and let stand 5 minutes. Garnish with Romano cheese.

Harvard Beets

    1 Tablespoon cornstarch
    1 1/2 teaspoon lemon juice
    1 cup apple juice
    dash ground cloves
    dash black pepper
    1 (16-ounce) can sliced beets, drained

In medium bowl, combine cornstarch, lemon juice, apple juice, cloves and pepper. Microwave on HIGH for 2-3 minutes until slightly thickened and bubbly, stirring each 1 minute during cooking.

Stir in beets and microwave on HIGH for 2 minutes until heated through.

Cheddar Cauliflower

    2 Tablespoons water
    1 medium head cauliflower, trimmed and cut into 4
      equal sized portions
    1 cup skim milk
    1 Tablespoon cornstarch
    1/2 teaspoon chicken bouillon granules
    1 teaspoon margarine
    dash black pepper
    1/2 cup shredded low-fat cheddar cheese

Arrange cauliflower in 2-quart casserole dish; sprinkle with water. Cover and cook on HIGH for 6-7 minutes until fork-tender, rotating dish once. Drain.

In a 2-cup measure, dissolve cornstarch in milk. Stir in remaining ingredients, except cheese. Microwave on HIGH for 2-3 minutes until thickened, stirring each 1 minute during cooking. Stir in cheese until melted. Pour cheese sauce over hot cauliflower.

Teriyaki Bell Peppers

2 large green bell peppers, seeded and cut in strips
1 large onion, sliced, rings separated
1 clove garlic, minced
1 Tablespoon white wine
1/2 teaspoon lemon juice
1 Tablespoon lite Teriyaki sauce
1 teaspoon olive oil

Combine ingredients in a 1 1/2-quart casserole dish. Cover and microwave on HIGH for 4-5 minutes, until tender-crisp, stirring once.

Squash with Herbs

5 small yellow crookneck squash, sliced
1 clove garlic, minced
1/2 teaspoon thyme
1/2 teaspoon basil
1/4 teaspoon rosemary
1/4 teaspoon black pepper
1 teaspoon margarine
1/4 cup shredded low-fat mozzarella cheese, as garnish
1 small diced tomato, for garnish

Place squash in a 2-quart casserole dish. Sprinkle remainder of ingredients, except tomato and cheese, over squash. Dot with margarine. Toss to mix. Cover and microwave on HIGH for 5-7 minutes until vegetables are tender. Sprinkle with cheese; allow to melt. Garnish with tomato.

Carrots and Peas in Cream Sauce

3 cups frozen peas and carrots
3 Tablespoons white wine
1 teaspoon all-purpose flour
1/2 cup plain fat-free yogurt
1/4 teaspoon garlic powder
1/4 teaspoon onion powder
1/4 teaspoon dill weed
1/2 teaspoon parsley flakes

Combine vegetables and wine in 1 1/2-quart casserole dish. Cover and microwave on HIGH for 6-8 minutes until tender, stirring once.

Sprinkle with flour and stir. Add remaining ingredients and cover. Microwave on MEDIUM (50% power) for 3-4 minutes until heated through, stirring twice.

Easy Potato and Mushroom Sauté

1 Tablespoon olive oil
1 medium onion, sliced, rings separated
1 (16-ounce) can whole potatoes, halved
1 (4-ounce) can sliced mushrooms, drained
1/8 teaspoon dried oregano
1/2 teaspoon parsley
dash black pepper

Combine olive oil and onion in 1 1/2-quart casserole dish. Cover and microwave on HIGH for 3-4 minutes until onions are soft. Stir in potatoes, mushrooms and seasonings. Cover and microwave on HIGH for 2-3 minutes until heated through.

Mediterranean Eggplant and Squash

serves 6

      1 medium eggplant, peeled, cut into 1/2-inch cubes
      1 medium red bell pepper, sliced into thin strips
      1 large yellow crookneck squash, cut into 1/4-inch
         thick slices
      1 clove garlic, minced
      1 teaspoon olive oil
      2 Tablespoons fresh minced parsley
      1/4 teaspoon dried basil
      6 pitted ripe olives, sliced
      2 Tablespoons crumbled feta cheese

In 2 1/2-quart casserole dish, combine eggplant, bell pepper, squash, garlic, oil, parsley and oil. Cover and microwave on HIGH for 9-11 minutes until vegetables are tender, stirring several times. Cover, stir in olives and basil, and cook on HIGH for 1-2 minutes more. Sprinkle with cheese.

Corn with Lime Juice and Taco Seasoning

      1 (16-ounce) package frozen corn
      1 Tablespoon fresh lime juice
      2 teaspoons olive oil
      2 teaspoons taco seasoning

Combine all ingredients in a 1 1/2-quart casserole dish. Cover and cook on HIGH for 9-10 minutes, stirring once.

Squash and Snow Pea Melange

      1 (1 1/2 pound) acorn squash
      1 clove garlic, minced
      2 Tablespoons margarine
      1/2 teaspoon dried parsley

1/2 teaspoon dried oregano
1/3 pound snow pea pods

Place squash in oven and microwave on HIGH for 2 minutes. Pierce skin deeply several times with a large fork. Microwave on HIGH for 5-6 minutes until tender, turning over, and rearranging twice. Allow to cool. Remove seed and membranes. Peel and cut into 1/2-inch slices.

Place garlic and margarine in a 2-quart baking dish. Microwave on HIGH for 30 seconds until margarine is melted. Add herbs and pea pods, and stir to coat. Cover pods with wax paper and cook on HIGH for 2-3 minutes until tender-crisp. Stir in cooked squash and microwave on HIGH for 1-2 minutes to heat through, stirring once.

New Potatoes with Dill

1 pound small new potatoes (washed, with a strip peeled around the center
1 Tablespoon olive oil
1 1/2 Tablespoons chopped fresh dill (or 1/2 teaspoon dried dill weed)

In a 2-quart casserole dish combine olive oil and potatoes. Cover and cook on HIGH for 6-8 minutes until tender, stirring twice. Sprinkle with dill and stir to coat.

Potato Mushroom Vegetable Medley

1 Tablespoon margarine
1 clove garlic
1/8 cup diced onion
1/8 teaspoon black pepper
1/2 cup chicken broth
4 small potatoes, cubed
1 cup sliced fresh mushrooms
1/2 cup broccoli florets
1 cup sliced crookneck squash

Combine margarine, garlic, onion, pepper and broth in 2 1/2-quart casserole dish. Cover and microwave on HIGH for 1 minute until onion is soft.

Stir in potatoes, mushrooms, broccoli and crookneck squash. Cover and microwave on HIGH for 7-9 minutes until vegetables are fork-tender, stirring twice.

Sweet Potatoes

> 3 medium (12-ounce) sweet potatoes, peeled and diced
> 1/4 cup apple juice
> 1 teaspoon ground cinnamon
> 1/8 teaspoon ground nutmeg
> 2 teaspoons margarine

In 1 1/2-quart casserole dish, combine sweet potatoes and apple juice. Sprinkle with cinnamon and nutmeg. Cover and cook on HIGH for 8-10 minutes until potatoes are tender. Dot with margarine.

Red-Skinned Potatoes and Zucchini

> 4 red-skinned potatoes, sliced
> 4 small zucchini, sliced
> 2 Tablespoons water
> 1 Tablespoon extra-virgin olive oil
> 1 teaspoon lemon juice
> 1 Tablespoon fresh parsley, chopped
> 1/2 teaspoon salt-free seasoning
> dash black pepper

Place potatoes, zucchini and water in a medium casserole dish. Cover and microwave on HIGH for 6-8 minutes until fork-tender, stirring twice. Drain.

Drizzle oil and lemon juice on potato mixture. Sprinkle with seasonings and gently toss.

Cream-Style Corn Bake

serves 6

> 1 (16-ounce) can cream-style corn
> 1/2 cup liquid egg substitute
> 2 Tablespoons diced green onion
> 2 Tablespoons diced celery
> 1/2 cup skim milk
> 1 teaspoon sugar
> 1/2 cup bread crumbs
> dash paprika

Coat a 2-quart baking dish with cooking spray. Mix together corn, egg substitute, onion, celery, milk, sugar and bread crumbs in prepared dish. Cover and microwave on MEDIUM (50% power) for 7 minutes. Stir. Increase level to MEDIUM HIGH (70% power) and cook for 4-5 minutes until a knife inserted in center comes out clean. Sprinkle with paprika.

Cauliflower and Broccoli Medley

> 2 Tablespoons water
> 2 cups fresh cauliflower florets
> 2 cups fresh broccoli florets
> 1 teaspoon salt-free seasoning
> dash white pepper

In a 2-quart casserole dish, mix together water and vegetables. Cover and microwave on HIGH for 5-7 minutes until vegetables are tender-crisp. Drain. Sprinkle with seasonings.

Snow Peas with Fresh Mint

> 2 teaspoons olive oil
> 1/4 cup thinly sliced celery
> 1/4 cup finely chopped red onion
> 3/4 cup frozen peas
> 1/4 pound snow peas, trimmed
> 1 Tablespoon chopped fresh mint

In a 2 1/2-quart casserole dish, combine olive oil, celery and onion. Cover and microwave on HIGH for 2 minutes. Stir in frozen peas, re-cover, and microwave on HIGH for 2 minutes. Stir in celery-onion mixture and microwave on HIGH for 1-2 minutes until snow peas are tender-crisp. Sprinkle with mint and serve.

Sautéed Mushrooms

> 3/4 pound small mushrooms, wiped clean, stems
>   removed
> 2 teaspoons margarine
> 1/2 teaspoon salt-free seasoning
> 1/8 teaspoon lemon-pepper
> 1/2 teaspoon lemon juice

Combine all ingredients in a 2-quart casserole dish. Microwave uncovered on HIGH for 1-2 minutes until just tender and heated through.

Seasoned Mashed Potatoes

1 1/4 pounds potatoes, peeled and cubed
3 cloves garlic, peeled
2 stalks celery, chopped into 1/2-inch pieces
1/4 cup water
1 Tablespoon olive oil
1/4-1/2 cup nonfat milk, warmed
1/2 teaspoon parsley flakes
1/4 teaspoon salt
1/8 teaspoon black pepper
paprika for garnish

In a 2 1/2-quart casserole dish, combine potatoes, garlic, celery and water. Cover with lid or vented plastic wrap. Cover and cook on HIGH for 8-10 minutes until fork-tender, stirring once.

With a slotted spoon, place potatoes, celery and garlic in mixing bowl. Beat with electric mixer. Pour in olive oil, milk, parsley, salt and pepper while continuing to beat. Increase speed and whip for 1 minute.

Transfer to serving bowl and garnish with paprika.

Lima Beans and Corn

2 cups frozen lima beans (or green beans)
2 cups frozen whole-kernel corn
1 Tablespoon water
1 teaspoon chicken bouillon granules
1 teaspoon margarine
1/2 teaspoon dried basil
1/8 teaspoon paprika

Combine all ingredients except paprika in a 2-quart casserole dish. Cover and cook on HIGH for 9-10 minutes until beans are tender-crisp, stirring once. Sprinkle with paprika.

Snow Peas and Red Pepper with Sesame Seeds

1 medium red bell pepper, sliced into strips
2 cups snow pea pods, trimmed
1 medium red onion, sliced thin, rings separated
2 Tablespoons low-salt soy sauce
2 teaspoons canola oil
2 Tablespoons sesame seeds
dash cayenne pepper

Combine all ingredients in a 2-quart casserole dish. Cover and cook on HIGH for 6-8 minutes until vegetables are tender crisp, stirring once.

Potatoes and Green Pepper Matchsticks

3 medium thin-skinned potatoes, thinly sliced
1 medium onion, thinly sliced, rings separated
1 medium green pepper, sliced into thin matchsticks.
2 Tablespoons water
1 teaspoon margarine
1/2 teaspoon parsley flakes
1/2 teaspoon garlic salt
1/8 teaspoon black pepper
2 Tablespoons grated Parmesan cheese

Combine all ingredients except cheese in a 2-quart casserole dish. Cover and cook on HIGH for 9-10 minutes, stirring twice. Sprinkle with cheese.

Teriyaki Broccoli

1 1/2 pounds fresh broccoli
1/4 cup water
1/2 cup Teriyaki sauce
1 Tablespoon fresh lemon juice
1/2 teaspoon ginger

Cut broccoli into florets leaving 2 inches of stalk. Place in 2 1/2-quart casserole dish and drizzle with water. Cover and cook on HIGH for 9-10 minutes, or until tender. Drain. Let stand 2 minutes.

Mix Teriyaki sauce, lemon juice, and ginger in a small bowl. Microwave on HIGH for 1-2 minutes until warm. Pour over broccoli and serve.

Herbed Corn on the Cob

1/2 teaspoon celery seed
1 teaspoon fresh dill, snipped
1/8 cup red bell pepper, diced
1/8 cup celery, diced
2 Tablespoons green onion, diced
1/2 cup bottled low-cal salad dressing with herbs
4 ears corn, husked

Mix all ingredients except corn in the bottom of a 8 x 12-inch baking dish. Roll ears of corn in the mixture to coat. Cover and microwave on HIGH for 9-10 minutes rearranging once. Let stand for 5 minutes.

New Potatoes with Green Onions in Olive Oil

1/4 cup water
1 pound new potatoes, scrubbed and quartered
2 Tablespoons olive oil
2 teaspoons red wine vinegar
1/4 teaspoon garlic powder
1/2 teaspoon dried parsley (or 1 Tablespoon fresh)
1/8 teaspoon pepper
2 green onions, chopped

Put water and potatoes in bottom of a casserole dish. Cover and microwave on HIGH for 6-10 minutes until potatoes are soft, rearranging once. Drain. Let stand 5 minutes.

In a medium bowl whisk remaining ingredients, then add potatoes to stand for 1 hour to blend flavors before serving. Reheating before serving optional.

Honey Carrots

> 4 cups thinly sliced carrots
> 1 small onion, sliced into rings
> 1 Tablespoon fresh chopped basil or 1/2 teaspoon dried basil
> 1 teaspoon honey
> 1 teaspoon margarine
> 1 teaspoon low-salt chicken bouillon granules

Mix all ingredients in bottom of 2-quart dish. Cover. Cook on HIGH for 7-10 minutes or until carrots are soft, stirring once.

Broccoli with Sunflower Seeds

> 2 Tablespoons water
> 3 cups broccoli florets
> 1 teaspoon lemon-pepper seasoning
> 2 teaspoons olive oil
> 2 Tablespoons sunflower seeds

Combine water, broccoli and seasoning in a 2-quart casserole dish. Cover and microwave on HIGH for 6-7 minutes until tender. Drain liquid. Drizzle with olive oil and sprinkle with sunflower seeds.

Carrot and Apple Bake

> 1/2 cup orange juice
> 1 Tablespoon honey
> 1 teaspoon dried parsley
> 4 medium carrots, thinly sliced
> 2 medium apples, cored, peeled and sliced

Place orange juice and honey in 2-cup measure. Microwave on HIGH for 45 seconds to thin honey.

Mix carrots and apples in a 2-quart casserole dish, pour orange juice mixture over top, and sprinkle with parsley. Cover and cook on HIGH for 8-10 minutes until carrots are tender, stirring once.

Black Eyed Peas and Cabbage

> 4 slices turkey-bacon, chopped
> 4 cups chopped cabbage
> 1 small onion, sliced and separated into rings
> 2 Tablespoons water
> 1/4 teaspoon dill weed
> 1 teaspoon chicken bouillon granules
> 1/8 teaspoon black pepper
> 2 cups cooked black eyed peas or 1 (15-ounce) can

Place turkey-bacon in 2 1/2-quart casserole dish. Cover and microwave on HIGH for 2-3 minutes until it begins crisping.

Add cabbage and onion. Sprinkle with water and seasonings. Cover and microwave on HIGH for 3 minutes. Add black eyed peas, stirring. Cover and cook an additional 2-6 minutes until heated through.

Country Spoon Bread with Poppy Seeds

Lovely paired with crab cakes.

> 2 Tablespoons margarine
> 1 1/2 cups nonfat milk
> 1/2 cup cornmeal
> 1/2 teaspoon dried thyme
> 2 teaspoons poppy seeds
> 1 cup sweet white corn, fresh or frozen
> 2 Tablespoons pimientos, drained, diced
> 1 teaspoon sugar
> 1/4 teaspoon salt
> 1/8 teaspoon cayenne pepper
> 3/4 cup liquid egg substitute, beaten

In a 2-quart casserole dish, combine all ingredients except the egg substitute. Cover with wax paper and microwave on HIGH for 6-7 minutes until cornmeal has absorbed most of the liquid, stirring each one minute for the last half of cooking time. Allow to cool for 10 minutes.

Slowly add 1/2 cup of the corn mixture to the eggs, mixing well to equalize temperatures. Slowly stir back into remaining corn mixture. Re-cover with wax paper and microwave on HIGH for 4 minutes, stirring once.

Smooth down the top of the mixture and reduce heat to MEDIUM (50% power). Microwave for 2-4 minutes until set. Let stand covered until serving time.

Barley and Walnut Pilaf

Great with fish!

> 1 Tablespoon olive oil
> 1 chopped onion
> 1 cup pearl barley
> 1/3 cup chopped walnuts
> 1 3/4 cups chicken broth
> 1 Tablespoon lemon juice
> 1/8 teaspoon black pepper
> 1/4 cup finely grated carrots

In a 2-quart casserole dish, combine the oil and onion. Cover and cook on HIGH for 2-3 minutes until tender-crisp. Add barley, stirring to coat each grain. Add walnuts, broth, lemon juice and pepper. Cover and microwave on HIGH for 5 minutes until liquid is boiling.

Reduce heat and microwave on MEDIUM (50% power) for 7-10 minutes until almost all liquid has been absorbed and barley is tender. Fold in carrots.

RICE/BEANS/GRAINS

Basic Brown Rice

> 2 1/2 cups water
> 1 cup brown rice

Combine water and rice in a 2 1/2-quart casserole dish. Cover and microwave on HIGH for 6-7 minutes. Reduce heat to MEDIUM LOW (30% power) and cook for 45 minutes until most of the liquid has been absorbed. Let stand 5 minutes.

Basic Cooked Dried Beans

> 1 1/2 cups (8 ounces) dried beans (black, pinto, navy, kidney, baby lima beans or black-eyed peas) rinsed and cleaned
> 6 cups water, divided

In 2-quart casserole stir together 3 cups water and beans. Cover and let soak 6 hours to overnight. Drain and rinse beans. Return to casserole and cover with 3 cups of water. Cover and cook on HIGH for 9 minutes, or until boiling, stirring once. Reduce heat to MEDIUM LOW (30% power) and let simmer for 40-45 minutes until beans are tender. Let stand 10 minutes.

White Beans

> 1 Tablespoon olive oil
> 2 cloves garlic, crushed
> 1 (16-ounce) can Great Northern beans, drained and rinsed
> 2 Tablespoons fresh parsley, finely chopped or 1 teaspoon dried parsley.

Combine oil and garlic in a 2-quart casserole dish. Cover and microwave on HIGH for 30 seconds. Stir in beans and cook, uncovered, for 2 1/2-3 minutes until heated through. Stir in parsley and cook an additional 45 seconds.

Brown Rice and Pearl Onions

> 2 teaspoons olive oil
> 2 green onions, thinly sliced
> 1 1/4 cups chicken broth
> 1 1/2 cups instant brown rice
> 1 (5-ounce) jar pearl onions
> 4 lemon slices, for garnish

Combine all ingredients except pearl onions and lemon in a 2-quart casserole dish. Cover and microwave on HIGH for 8 minutes until rice is soft and liquid has been absorbed. Stir in pearl onions and let stand, covered, 5 minutes. Garnish with lemon wedges.

Rosemary and Mushroom Wild Rice

> 1 teaspoon olive oil
> 1/2 cup chopped celery
> 4 ounces fresh sliced mushrooms
> 3 cups chicken broth
> 1 cup wild rice
> 1/4 teaspoon dried rosemary

Combine all ingredients in a 3-quart casserole dish. Cover and cook on HIGH for 6-7 minutes. Reduce heat to MEDIUM LOW (30% power) and cook an additional 30 minutes until liquid has been absorbed. Drain. Let stand covered for 5 minutes.

Rice Cooked in Cream of Mushroom Soup

> 1 1/2 cups dry instant rice
> 1 cup diced green pepper
> 3 Tablespoons chopped pimiento
> 1 1/2 cups sliced mushrooms
> 1 cup condensed low-fat cream of mushroom soup
> 1 cup skim milk

Combine all ingredients in 2 1/2-quart casserole dish. Cover and cook on HIGH for 6 minutes until rice is done and vegetables are tender, stirring twice.

Oriental Snow Peas, Mushrooms and Rice

1 1/2 cups dry instant rice
2 cups snow peas, frozen, thawed
1 cup sliced fresh mushrooms
2/3 cup water
2 cloves garlic, minced
1/4 teaspoon ground ginger
2 Tablespoons lite soy sauce

Combine all ingredients in a 2 1/2-quart casserole dish. Cover and microwave on HIGH for 6-9 minutes, until rice is done and snow peas are tender-crisp, stirring twice.

Steamed Rice with Fresh Parsley

1 cup uncooked white rice
2 cups water
1/2 teaspoon chicken bouillon granules
3 Tablespoons chopped fresh parsley

In 2-quart casserole dish, mix rice, water and bouillon. Cover and microwave on HIGH for 5 minutes. Reduce setting to MEDIUM (50% power) and cook for 15 minutes. Fluff with fork and stir in parsley.

Pureed Black Beans with Green Chile

1 (16-ounce) can black beans
1 small onion, chopped
1 clove garlic, minced
1/2 teaspoon ground cumin
3 Tablespoons canned chopped green chile
1/8 teaspoon cayenne pepper
1/2 teaspoon beef bouillon granules
1/2 cup hot water
1 small tomato, seeded and chopped for garnish

Puree all ingredients, except tomato, in a blender. Place in a 1 1/2-quart casserole dish. Cover and microwave on HIGH for 2 minutes. Stir and reduce power to MEDIUM HIGH (70% power). Microwave for an additional 3-5 minutes until heated through. Garnish with tomato.

Confetti Rice Molds

> 1 3/4 cup water
> 1/4 teaspoon salt
> 1 cup long-grain rice
> 1/2 red-bell pepper, cut into 1/4-inch pieces
> 1/2 green bell pepper, cut into 1/4-inch pieces
> 1/2 cup frozen corn
> 4 lettuce leaves

Combine water, salt and rice in a 2-quart casserole dish. Cover tightly and microwave on HIGH for 3-4 minutes until boiling. Reduce heat to MEDIUM (50% power) and cook for 8-10 minutes until liquid has been absorbed. Add the peppers and corn, stirring, and microwave on HIGH an additional 1 1/2 minutes. Let stand 5 minutes.

Spoon 1/4 of rice mixture into a custard cup. Pack rice down with a spoon. Place lettuce leaves on serving plate and invert rice mold over lettuce. Repeat with remaining rice.

Green Bean Wild Rice

> 3 Tablespoons olive oil
> 1 clove garlic, minced
> 1/2 cup onion, chopped
> 1/2 cup green onion, chopped
> 1 cup wild rice
> 3 cups chicken broth
> 1 pound green beans, trimmed, cut into 1 1/2-inch
>   pieces
> 1 teaspoon salt-free seasoning

In 3-quart casserole dish combine oil, garlic and onion. Cover and microwave on HIGH for 2-3 minutes until onion is tender. Stir in rice to coat. Add broth, green beans, and seasoning. Cover and microwave on HIGH for 5-7 minutes, until boiling. Reduce heat to MEDIUM LOW and cook for 30-40 minutes until green beans and rice are tender and liquid is absorbed.

Rice Pilaf with Pecans and Broccoli

 1 1/2 Tablespoons margarine
 1 medium onion, finely chopped
 1 cup white rice
 2 1/4 cups chicken broth
 1 cup long thin broccoli florets
 1 teaspoon water
 1/4 cup chopped pecans

In a 2 1/2-quart casserole dish combine margarine and onion.
Cook on HIGH for 2-3 minutes until onion is tender. Add rice,
coating each grain. Add broth and stir. Cover tightly and
microwave on HIGH for 4-6 minutes, until boiling. Reduce heat
to MEDIUM LOW (30% power) and microwave for 20 minutes.
Let stand covered 5 minutes.

While rice is standing, place broccoli in a shallow microwaveable
dish. Sprinkle with water, cover, and microwave on HIGH for 2-
3 minutes until fork-tender. Drain. Add broccoli and nuts to rice
and mix well. Covered rice can retain heat for up to 1 hour
before serving.

Mexicali Rice with Green Chile and Cilantro

 1 Tablespoon olive oil
 1 small chopped onion
 1 clove garlic, minced
 1/2 bell pepper diced
 2 Tablespoons pimientos, chopped
 1 small fresh serrano chile, minced
 2 cups instant brown rice
 2 cups hot water
 2 teaspoons low-salt chicken bouillon granules
 1/4 cup fresh chopped parsley
 2 Tablespoons fresh chopped cilantro

In a 2-quart casserole, combine oil, onion, garlic, bell pepper,
pimiento, and serrano chile. Cover and microwave on HIGH for
3-4 minutes until tender-crisp.

Dissolve bouillon granules into hot water and add to vegetables,
stirring. Add the rice and parsley and microwave on HIGH for

8-10 minutes until rice is done. Let stand 5 minutes. Fluff with a fork and garnish with cilantro.

Colorful Basmati Rice

> 1 3/4 cups water
> 1 cup basmati rice
> 1 cup frozen mixed vegetables (corn, peas, cubed
>   carrots)
> 1 teaspoon salt-free seasoning

Combine ingredients in a 2-quart casserole dish. Cover and microwave on HIGH for 4-6 minutes until boiling.

Reduce heat to MEDIUM (50% power) and microwave an additional 5-6 minutes until water is absorbed and rice is tender. Let stand 5 minutes.

Refried Beans

> 1 (16-ounce) can fat-free refried beans
> 1/4 cup seeded, chopped tomato, for garnish
> 2 Tablespoons diced fresh parsley, for garnish

Place beans in a round 1 1/2-quart casserole dish. Spoon beans out of center to form a cavity to allow faster, more even heating of beans. Cover and microwave on HIGH for 2 1/2-4 minutes. Spoon into serving dish and garnish with tomato and parsley.

Chili Rellenos with Refried Beans

> 2 (7-ounce) cans whole green chiles
> 3/4 cup canned vegetarian-style refried beans
> 1/2 cup liquid egg substitute
> 3 Tablespoons all-purpose flour
> 1/2 teaspoon baking powder
> dash black pepper
> 1/2 teaspoon vegetable oil
> 1/3 cup low-fat grated Cheddar cheese
> 1/4 teaspoon paprika, for garnish

Slit chili peppers lengthwise and remove seeds. Fill each with even amount of the refried beans. Pour egg substitute into a small bowl and whisk. Into another small bowl, combine flour, baking powder, and pepper. Lightly coat bottom of a baking dish with the oil. Dip stuffed chiles in egg mixture, then in flour mixture and arrange on coated dish with space between each chile.

Leave uncovered and microwave on HIGH for 3-4 minutes to set the eggs and to heat through. Garnish with cheese and paprika and microwave on HIGH for one minute to melt cheese.

Black Bean Enchiladas

> 1 medium onion, chopped
> 2 cloves garlic, minced
> 1 (16-ounce) can crushed tomatoes
> 1 Tablespoon cornstarch
> 1 serrano or jalapeño pepper, minced
> 1/2 teaspoon ground cumin
> 2 cups cooked black beans or 1 (15-ounce) can black
>   beans, rinsed and drained
> 1/2 cup plain low-fat yogurt
> 8 (6 inch) corn tortillas
> 1/3 cup shredded low-fat Cheddar cheese

Combine onion and garlic in a 2-quart casserole dish. Cover and microwave on HIGH for 2 1/2 minutes. Blend cornstarch with a few Tablespoons of juice from crushed tomatoes and add to onions. Add remainder of crushed tomatoes, pepper and cumin. Cook on HIGH for 4-5 minutes until bubbly, stirring each 1 minute. Set aside.

In a medium bowl, combine beans and yogurt. Soften tortillas by wrapping in slightly damp paper towel and microwaving on HIGH for 1 minute. Spread 1/8 of bean mixture on lower third of each tortilla and roll up.

Place enchiladas seam-side down in 8 x 12-inch baking dish. Cover with sauce and cook on HIGH for 4-6 minutes until heated through. Sprinkle with cheese and cook an additional minute to melt cheese.

Hopping John

"Southerners' New Year Good Luck Dish"

> 1/4 cup chopped onion
> 1/4 cup white vinegar
> 1 1/2 cups instant brown rice
> 1 1/4 cups water
> 1 1/4 cups chopped onion
> 3 cloves garlic, minced
> 1 teaspoon dried oregano
> 1/4 teaspoon hot sauce
> 2/3 cup diced smoked cooked turkey
> 1 (15-ounce) can black-eyed peas

Combine 1/4 cup chopped onion and vinegar. Let stand 30 minutes. Drain and set aside. Will be used as garnish.

Combine rice, water, 1 1/4 cups onion, garlic, oregano and hot sauce in medium pan. Cover and cook on HIGH 8-10 minutes. Add turkey and black-eyed peas, stirring. Cover and cook on HIGH another 2-3 minutes. Let stand 5 minutes. Garnish with vinegar marinated onions and serve.

Vegetable Paella

> 1 teaspoon olive oil
> 1 small onion
> 3 cloves garlic, minced
> 1 cup thin asparagus, cut into 1-inch pieces
> 2 small red-skinned potatoes, thinly sliced
> 1 1/2 cups instant brown rice
> 2 cups hot vegetable or chicken broth
> 3/4 teaspoons oregano
> 1 teaspoon saffron (optional)
> 1 cup frozen, thawed peas
> 1/2 cup diced tomato
> 1 (6-ounce) jar marinated artichoke heart pieces
> 8 pitted olives

Combine olive oil, onion, garlic, asparagus, and potatoes in large casserole dish. Cover and cook on HIGH for 6-8 minutes until potatoes are almost completely tender.

Add rice, broth, spices, peas, tomatoes, artichoke and olives. Stir well. Cover and cook on HIGH for 10-12 minutes until rice and potatoes are done. Let stand 5 minutes.

Vegetarian Chili

>   1 green bell pepper, chopped
>   1 large onion, chopped
>   3 cloves garlic, minced
>   2 teaspoons chili powder
>   1 teaspoon cumin
>   2 bay leaves
>   1/2 teaspoon oregano
>   dash cayenne pepper
>   1/4 cup bulgur
>   1 1/2 cups water
>   2 teaspoons low-salt soy sauce
>   1 (15 1/2-ounce) can tomatoes, chopped
>   1 (15-ounce) can kidney beans, rinsed and drained

In a 3-quart casserole dish, combine onion and garlic. Cover and microwave on HIGH for 3-4 minutes until tender.

Stir in remainder of ingredients. Cover and cook on HIGH for 7 minutes. Reduce heat to MEDIUM LOW (30% power) and simmer for 20-25 minutes.

PASTA

Tomato Mushroom Sauce with Spiral Pasta

yields 8 cups

Use half and freeze the rest for a later meal.

> 4 cups cooked pasta
> 1 Tablespoon olive oil
> 1 large onion, chopped
> 4 large garlic cloves, minced
> 1 cup diced carrots
> 1 pound sliced fresh mushrooms
> 1 (14-ounce) can tomato sauce
> 1 (14-ounce) can tomatoes, drained, chopped
> 2 Tablespoons tomato paste
> 1 teaspoon dried oregano
> 1 teaspoon dried basil
> 1 teaspoon paprika
> 1/2 cup minced fresh Italian parsley
> dash salt
> dash black pepper
> dash cayenne

Cook pasta according to package directions on conventional stove top. Meanwhile, in a deep 3-quart casserole dish, combine oil, onion, garlic, and carrots. Microwave on HIGH for 3-4 minutes until tender-crisp.

Stir in mushrooms and microwave on HIGH for 4-5 minutes. Stir in tomato sauce, tomatoes, tomato paste and seasonings. Microwave uncovered on HIGH for 5 minutes. Reduce heat to MEDIUM LOW (30% power) and microwave an additional 20 minutes.

Linguine with Zucchini and Tomatoes

> 4-5 cups cooked linguine
> 3 medium zucchini, quartered lengthwise, cut into 1/2-
>   inch wedges
> 2 Tablespoons water
> 1 Tablespoon olive oil

1/4 teaspoon dried oregano
4 small tomatoes, chopped
4 Tablespoons minced fresh basil, or 2 teaspoons dried
    basil
1 teaspoon salt-free seasoning
dash cayenne pepper
1/4 teaspoon paprika

Cook linguine according to package directions on conventional stove top. Meanwhile, combine zucchini, water, olive oil, and oregano in a 2 1/2-quart casserole. Cover and microwave on HIGH for 5-6 minutes until tender-crisp, stirring twice.

Place hot cooked pasta in a large serving bowl. Add tomatoes, zucchini, basil, and seasonings. Toss well.

Eggplant and Yellow Tomato with Spaghetti

4-5 cups cooked spaghetti
1 large eggplant, unpeeled, diced to 1/2-inch cubes
1/2 teaspoon salt
2 Tablespoons olive oil
1 large clove garlic, minced
1 large red bell pepper, diced
3 large yellow tomatoes, chopped
10 Calamata olives, coarsely chopped

Prepare spaghetti according to package directions on conventional stove top. Meanwhile, place eggplant in colander. Sprinkle with salt. Let drain for 15-30 minutes. Rinse with cold water and blot dry with paper towel.

Place eggplant in a deep 3-quart casserole dish. Drizzle with olive oil. Microwave uncovered on HIGH for 5 minutes. Stir, reduce heat to MEDIUM (50% power) and microwave an additional 5-10 minutes until soft, stirring twice. Stir in bell pepper, tomatoes and garlic. Cook uncovered on HIGH for 5 minutes, stirring once. Stir in olives and microwave an additional 1 minute. Serve over hot cooked spaghetti.

Pasta Primavera

> 4-5 cups cooked linguine
> 1 cup frozen peas
> 1 pound thin fresh asparagus, trimmed and cut in 1-inch pieces
> 2 cups chopped zucchini
> 1/4 cup red bell pepper, chopped
> 1 Tablespoon olive oil
> 2 Tablespoons fresh basil, chopped, or 1 teaspoon dried
> 4 Tablespoons fresh parsley, chopped or 2 teaspoons dried
> 1 cup spinach leaves, thinly slivered
> 1 teaspoon salt-free seasoning
> dash black pepper

Prepare linguine according to package directions on conventional stove top. Meanwhile, combine peas, asparagus, zucchini, and bell pepper in a 2 1/2-quart casserole dish. Drizzle with olive oil. Cover and microwave on HIGH for 8-10 minutes until vegetables are tender-crisp, stirring twice. Drain well. Blot dry with a paper towel.

Combine cooked vegetables, hot cooked pasta, basil, parsley and spinach in a large serving bowl. Add seasonings and gently mix. Serve hot.

Asian Broccoli and Snow Pea Pasta

> 4-5 cups cooked linguine
> 3 cups broccoli florets
> 1 cup snow peas
> 2 Tablespoons water
> 1/4 teaspoon low-salt soy sauce
> 1 Tablespoon sesame oil
> 1 Tablespoon sesame seeds
> 3 cups cucumbers, cut into slivers
> 2 Tablespoons green onion, chopped

Cook linguine according to package directions on conventional stove top. Meanwhile, place broccoli, snow peas and water in a 2

1/2-quart casserole dish. Cover and cook on HIGH for 6-8 minutes until vegetables are just tender, stirring twice. Drain. In a small bowl, mix together soy sauce oil, and sesame seeds.

In a large shallow serving bowl, combine cucumbers, green onion, cooked vegetables, soy sauce-sesame mixture, and hot cooked linguine. Toss well.

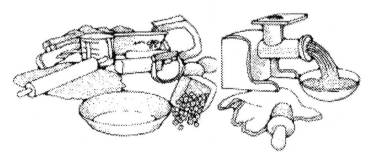

Fettuccine with Creamy Asparagus

1 1/2 pounds thick asparagus, trimmed, cut in 1-inch segments
1 Tablespoon olive oil
2 Tablespoons water
1/8 cup minced green onion
2 cups sliced mushrooms
1/4 cup low-fat sour cream
dash black pepper
pinch tarragon
1 pound fettuccine, cooked

Cook fettuccine according to package directions on conventional stove top. Meanwhile, place asparagus in a 2 1/2-quart casserole dish, drizzle with oil and water. Cover and cook on HIGH for 6-8 minutes until tender-crisp, stirring twice. (If using thin asparagus, reduce cooking time.)

Add onion and mushrooms to asparagus. Cover and cook on HIGH for 4-5 minutes until mushrooms are tender. Add sour cream, pepper, tarragon and hot cooked fettuccine. Stir gently. Cover and cook on MEDIUM (50% power) for 3-4 minutes until heated through.

Spaghetti with Wild Mushrooms

3/4 pound uncooked spaghetti, or other pasta
1 pound porcini, shiitake or chanterelle mushrooms,
cleaned and sliced
1 Tablespoon olive oil
1 Tablespoon margarine
1/2 teaspoon fresh lemon juice

Cook spaghetti according to package instructions on conventional stove top. Meanwhile, combine mushrooms, oil, margarine and lemon juice in a 3-quart casserole dish. Microwave on HIGH for 5-6 minutes until tender, stirring twice.

Drain spaghetti, toss with mushroom mixture, and serve.

SEAFOOD

Salmon Steaks

serves 2

>2 (6-ounce) salmon steaks, 3/4-inch thick
>1 Tablespoon olive oil
>1 Tablespoon lemon juice
>1 teaspoon Worcestershire sauce
>1/4 teaspoon dried oregano
>1/2 teaspoon paprika
>1/2 teaspoon dill weed

Brush salmon steaks with olive oil and sprinkle one side of the fish with half of the lemon, Worcestershire sauce, oregano, paprika and dill. Cover and microwave on MEDIUM (50% power) for 4 minutes until fish is slightly firm and milky liquid comes to the surface.

Rearrange and turn over steaks. Sprinkle with remaining lemon juice and herbs. Cover and microwave on MEDIUM for 3-5 minutes until just cooked through.

Fish Stew

>1 small chopped onion
>1 1/2 cups low-salt chicken broth
>1 (15-ounce) can whole tomatoes, liquid reserved for
>   another use, tomatoes cut into quarters
>2 ears corn on the cob, cut into 1 1/2-inch pieces
>1 cup cauliflower, cut into 1-inch pieces
>1 teaspoon salt-free seasoning
>1 pound cooked fish fillets or steaks
>1 medium zucchini, cut into 1-inch pieces

In a 2 1/2-quart casserole dish, place onion, cover, and microwave on HIGH for 2 minutes until tender. Add broth, tomatoes, corn, cauliflower and seasoning. Cover and cook on HIGH for 10-15 minutes until vegetables are just tender, stirring twice.

Break fish into pieces and add to casserole along with zucchini. Cover and microwave on HIGH for 3-4 minutes until fish is cooked through.

Mussels in Tomato Sauce and Wine

2 pounds mussels, cleaned and scrubbed
2 teaspoons olive oil
1 medium onion, sliced into rings
1 large clove garlic, crushed or minced
3 1/2 cups spaghetti sauce
1/4 cup dry white wine
1 teaspoon dried basil
1 teaspoon dried oregano
2 bay leaves

To clean shrimp, discard any open or extra heavy shells. Remove any beard with a knife. Scrub and wash the shells in several changes of cold water. The last rinse before using should come out clean. Set aside.

Combine olive oil, onion and garlic in 3-quart casserole dish. Cover and cook on HIGH for 2-3 minutes until tender-crisp. Stir in spaghetti sauce, wine and herbs. Cover and cook on HIGH for 5-6 minutes until beginning to boil, stirring once.

Add mussels, re-cover, and cook on HIGH for 4-6 minutes until mussels are open, stirring after 3 minutes. Discard any unopened shells.

Nicoise Salad

ever popular.

2 Tablespoons water
1/2 pound green beans, trimmed, cut into 2-inch pieces
3 small red-skinned potatoes, cut into 3/4-inch cubes
1/2 cup red onion, thinly sliced
1 (8-ounce) can water packed tuna, flaked
1 (6-ounce) jar artichoke hearts, drained and halved
1 Tablespoon red wine vinegar
2 Tablespoons olive oil
4 cups salad greens
dash black pepper

Place water and green beans in a 2-quart casserole dish. Cover and microwave on HIGH for 4-5 minutes until tender. Rinse beans in cold water, drain, and set aside in a large bowl.

Place potatoes in the casserole dish. Cover and cook on HIGH for 6-7 minutes until tender. Rinse in cold water, drain, and add to bowl with beans. Add onions, tuna and artichoke to beans and potatoes. Whisk together vinegar and oil in a small bowl. Pour over vegetables and toss well. Add salad greens and toss well. Sprinkle with pepper.

Fish Fillets with Parsley and Walnut Sauce

> 1 pound fish fillets (orange roughy, cod or halibut)
> 2 Tablespoons fresh lemon juice
> 1 1/2 Tablespoons olive oil
> 1/2 cup hot water
> 1 teaspoon vegetable bouillon powder
> 1 cup coarsely chopped walnuts
> 1/2 cup fresh parsley
> dash salt
> dash black pepper
> 4 parsley leaves, for garnish

Arrange fish in a 9 x 12-inch baking dish, leaving space between each, and tucking under any very thin ends. Sprinkle with lemon juice. Cover and microwave on MEDIUM for 8-12 minutes until fish flakes easily with a fork. Let stand, covered, 5 minutes.

In a medium bowl, dissolve vegetable bouillon in water. Whisk in oil. Stir in walnuts and parsley, salt and pepper. Cook on HIGH for 2 minutes until heated through.

To serve, place fish on individual plates and spoon sauce over fish. Place a parsley leaf on each.

Oriental Shrimp with Snow Peas and Sprouts

1 Tablespoon sesame oil
2 cloves garlic, minced
3/4 pound snow peas, trimmed
3/4 pound fresh bean sprouts
3 green onions, cut into 1-inch pieces
1 1/2 pounds medium-size peeled shrimp
2 1/2 Tablespoons low-salt soy sauce
2 teaspoons grated fresh ginger
2 teaspoons orange juice

Place garlic and oil in a round 2 1/2-quart casserole dish and microwave on HIGH for 30 seconds.

Toss peas, sprouts and onions in garlic mixture to coat. Move the vegetables into the center, leaving a 2-inch pathway around the outer edge of dish. Arrange the shrimp in this pathway.

In a small bowl, combine soy sauce, ginger and orange juice. Drizzle over shrimp and vegetables. Cover with wax paper and cook on HIGH for 5-7 minutes until shrimp are cooked through, stirring vegetables once and removing any smaller shrimp as soon as they are done.

Fish and Red Pepper Salad

1 pound cooked white fish fillets, flaked
1/2 cup low-fat mayonnaise, or mayonnaise substitute
1/4 cup finely chopped green onion
1 teaspoon lemon juice
1 red bell pepper, diced
1/4 teaspoon dried dill weed
1/8 teaspoon black pepper

Mix together all ingredients and chill. Serve on a bed of salad greens, or on soft whole wheat rolls as a sandwich.

Fish Fillets with Salsa

1 pound fish fillets (orange roughy, cod or halibut)
1 cup mild fresh salsa

Place fillets in a 12 x 8-inch baking dish. Tuck under any very thin ends. Pour salsa over fish. Cover and microwave on HIGH for 4-6 minutes until fish flakes easily with a fork.

Louisiana Shrimp

2 stalks celery, finely chopped
1 bell pepper, finely chopped
1 large onion, finely chopped
1/2 Tablespoons olive oil
2 cloves garlic
1 (4-ounce) can sliced mushrooms, drained
1 (14 1/2-ounce) can low-salt stewed tomatoes
1/2 pound fresh or frozen shrimp, shelled
1 cup cooked red beans
1/2 teaspoon salt-free seasoning
1/4 teaspoon pepper
1/4 teaspoon liquid red-pepper seasoning
1 teaspoon Worcestershire sauce

In a 2-quart casserole, combine celery, pepper, onion, oil and garlic. Cover and cook on HIGH for 7-8 minutes until vegetables are tender. Stir in remaining ingredients. Cover and cook on HIGH for 2 minutes then reduce power setting to MEDIUM (50% power) and cook an additional 3-4 minutes until test done.

Seafood Broccoli Bake

8-12 ounces imitation crab meat
1 1/2 cups broccoli florets
1/4 cup chopped pimiento
1/2 cup cauliflower, chopped
1 small red onion, sliced into rings
2 cups liquid egg substitute
1/4 teaspoon black pepper
1 teaspoon parsley flakes
1/2 cup grated fat-free Cheddar cheese

Arrange seafood, broccoli, pimento, cauliflower and onion on bottom of a large shallow baking dish. Pour egg substitute over top. Sprinkle with seasoning. Cover and cook on HIGH for 6-8 minutes until vegetables are tender and eggs are set. Sprinkle cheese on top and cook on HIGH an additional 15 seconds to melt cheese.

White Fish with Julienne Vegetables

> 4 small potatoes
> 2 small crookneck squash
> 2 carrot
> 1 medium zucchini
> 2 teaspoons margarine
> dash celery salt
> 1/4 teaspoon pepper
> 1/4 teaspoon thyme
> 1/2 teaspoon onion powder
> 1 Tablespoon white wine
> 1 pound 1/2-inch thick or less white fish fillets.

Cut vegetables julienne-style and arrange in baking dish. Dot with margarine. Sprinkle with seasonings and wine. Place fish fillets on top. Cover and microwave on HIGH for 6-9 minutes, rotating dish twice.

Fish Fillets with Teriyaki Sauce

> 1 pound white fish fillets
> 1/4 cup low-salt Teriyaki sauce
> 1 teaspoon lemon juice
> 1/2 teaspoon garlic powder
> 1/4 teaspoon black pepper

Place fillets in a single layer in a 12 x 8-inch baking dish, folding under any very thin ends to avoid overcooking. Pour sauce over fish and sprinkle with lemon and seasonings. Cover and microwave on HIGH for 3-5 minutes until fish flakes easily with a fork.

Lorraine's Onion Smothered Orange Roughy

> 1 pound Orange roughy fillets (or other type fish fillets)
> 2 teaspoons lecithin granules (or 2 teaspoons olive oil)
> 1 medium onion sliced into rings
> 1/2 teaspoon lemon-herb or lemon-pepper prepared seasoning
> 1/2 teaspoon garlic powder
> 1/2 teaspoon onion powder
> 1/2 lemon cut into thin slices

In bottom of shallow baking dish spread onion rings and sprinkle 1 teaspoon lecithin granules (or one teaspoon olive oil). Coat fish with lemon seasoning, garlic powder and onion powder. Place over onions and top with remaining lecithin (or olive oil) and lemon slices.

Cover and cook on MEDIUM HIGH (70% power) for 6-9 minutes or until test done, rearranging half way through cooking time. Fish is done when it flakes easily with a fork. Let stand 5 minutes.

Mushroom Scallops with Cheese-Crumb Topping

> 1 small onion, finely chopped
> 1/2 cup celery, finely sliced
> 1 Tablespoon pimiento, chopped
> 8 ounces fresh mushrooms, sliced
> 1 clove garlic, minced
> 1/4 cup white wine
> 1 Tablespoon lemon juice
> 1 teaspoon Dijon mustard
> 1/2 teaspoon low-salt chicken bouillon granule
> 1 Tablespoon all-purpose flour
> 1 pound scallops, halved
>
> Topping
> 2 Tablespoons bread crumbs
> 2 Tablespoons grated Parmesan cheese
> 1/4 teaspoon dried oregano
> 1 teaspoon dried basil

In bottom of a 2 1/2 quart baking dish combine all ingredients except topping ingredients. Cover and cook on MEDIUM (50% power) for 7-12 minutes, stirring every 2 minutes. Scallops are done when opaque and flake easily.

In small bowl, mix together bread crumbs, Parmesan cheese, oregano and basil. Top scallops with crumb mixture. Heat uncovered for 1-2 minutes on MEDIUM. Serve.

Easy Italian Seasoned Fish

1/2 cup bottled low-fat Caesar dressing
1 cup Italian seasoned bread crumbs
1 pound fish fillets

Brush fish with Caesar dressing. Dip in bread crumbs. Place in baking dish and fold under any very thin ends to avoid overcooking. Cover with wax paper and microwave on HIGH for 4-6 minutes, rearranging after 2 minutes. Fish is done when it flakes easily with a fork.

Zesty Marinated Fish

2 Tablespoons olive oil
1/4 teaspoon salt
1 clove crushed garlic
1/3 cup tomato sauce
1/2 teaspoon chili powder
1/8 teaspoon oregano
1/2 teaspoon Worcestershire sauce
1 pound fish fillets

In a small bowl, combine all ingredients except fish. Pour into a plastic bag. Add the fish and marinate in the refrigerator for 30-60 minutes, turning bag over once.

Arrange fish in a baking dish, tucking under any very thin ends. Cover, and microwave on HIGH for 3-5 minutes, rearranging after half the time.

Seafood Nuggets

> 1 pound fresh or thawed frozen shark, cut into 1 inch
>   cubes
> 1/2 cup low-fat Italian salad dressing
> 1/3 cup bread crumbs
> 1/3 cup low fat Romano cheese
> 1 teaspoon parsley flakes
> 1/2 teaspoon paprika
> lemon wedges to garnish

Rinse shark, pat dry. Pour dressing into a small bowl. Combine
bread crumbs, cheese, parsley and paprika in a pie plate. Dip
shark in dressing, then roll in crumb mixture to coat.

Arrange shark on a plate. Microwave, uncovered, on HIGH for 2
minutes. Rearrange, moving inside pieces to outside of dish.
Microwave on HIGH for 1-2 minutes until test done. Garnish
with lemon.

Stuffed Cod

> 1 teaspoon margarine
> 1 cup sliced fresh mushrooms
> 1/2 cup finely chopped green onion
> 3/4 cup Italian-seasoned bread crumbs
> 1/4 cup liquid-egg substitute
> 1 clove garlic, minced
> 2 Tablespoons lemon juice
> 1 pound cod fillets (may substitute sole, orange roughy
>   or flounder)
> 1 teaspoon parsley flakes
> dash paprika

Rinse fillets. Pat dry. Brush both sides with lemon juice. Set aside in refrigerator.

In mixing bowl, place margarine and microwave on HIGH for 20 seconds to soften. Mix in mushrooms and onion and cook on HIGH for 2-3 minutes until vegetables are tender-crisp. Stir in bread crumbs, egg substitute, and garlic.

Spread filling mixture on each cod fillet to 1/2-inch of the edges. Roll up fillets and fasten with toothpick. Place seam side down in 8-inch square baking dish. Sprinkle with parsley and paprika. Cover with wax paper and microwave on HIGH for 7-9 minutes until fish flakes easily with a fork.

Easy Herb Fish

> 1/2 cup bottled low-fat Italian salad dressing
> 1 cup crushed low-fat cracker crumbs
> 1 pound fish fillets
> 1/2 teaspoon dried dill weed
> 1/2 teaspoon dried majoram

Brush fish with Italian dressing. Dip in cracker crumbs and herbs. Place in baking dish and fold under any very thin ends to prevent over cooking. Cover with wax paper and microwave on HIGH for 4-6 minutes, rearranging after 2 minutes. Fish is done when it flakes easily with a fork.

Halibut and Asparagus Dinner

> 1/2 pound halibut fillets
> 1/2 pound asparagus spears, trimmed
> 1/2 lemon
> 1 teaspoon salt-free seasoning

Place asparagus on bottom of baking dish. Arrange fish on top. Sprinkle with lemon juice and seasoning. Cover and cook on HIGH for 4-5 minutes until thickest portion of fillet is 99 opaque. Let stand 5 minutes.

Fish Fillets with Onion-Mustard Dressing

> 2 Tablespoons nonfat yogurt
> 2 Tablespoons Dijon mustard
> 2 Tablespoons low-calorie Italian dressing
> 1/2 cup chopped onion
> 1/8 teaspoon coarse ground pepper
> 1/4 cup pine nuts
> 1 pound fish fillets

Mix together first 6 ingredients in a small bowl. Set aside.

Arrange fish in baking dish, tucking under any very thin ends to avoid overcooking. Cover with wax paper and microwave on HIGH for 3-6 minutes, repositioning dish in oven once to ensure even cooking. Fish is done when it flakes easily with a fork. Let stand 3 minutes.

Cook onion-mustard sauce on MEDIUM (50% power) for 3-4 minutes until heated. Spoon over fish and serve.

Marinated Shark with Bell Peppers and Tomatoes

> 1 pound shark, cut into 1 inch cubes
> 1 large green bell pepper, cut into 1-inch pieces
> 1 medium onion, cut into wedges
> 2/3 pound cherry tomatoes
> 4 Tablespoons low-salt soy sauce
> 2 teaspoons lemon juice
> 1/2 teaspoons garlic powder

Place shark, bell pepper, onion and tomatoes in a plastic bag. In small bowl, combine soy sauce, lemon juice, garlic powder. Pour soy sauce mixture into bag with shark and vegetables. Marinate in refrigerator for one-half hour, turning bag over once.

Pour shark-vegetable mixture into baking dish. Cover. Cook on HIGH for 5-7 minutes, stirring once, until shark is done and vegetables are tender-crisp.

Fish and Rice

1 1/2 cups instant rice, brown or white
1/2 cup chopped onion
1/2 cup diced red bell pepper
1 Tablespoon dried basil
1/2 teaspoon dried parsley
1/4 teaspoon low-salt chicken bouillon granules
2 Tablespoons lemon juice
1 1/4 cups water
1 pound fish fillets
1 Tablespoon margarine
dash paprika

In baking dish combine rice, onion, bell pepper, basil, parsley, chicken bouillon, lemon juice, and water. Stir well.

Arrange fish evenly over rice, overlapping any very thin ends. Dot with margarine. Sprinkle with paprika.

Cover and cook on HIGH for 10-12 minutes, rearranging fish after half the time. Let stand, covered, 5 minutes.

Halibut Steaks Parmesan

1 pound halibut steaks
2 Tablespoons white wine
1 Tablespoon olive oil
1/4 teaspoon dried oregano leaves (or 3/4 teaspoons fresh oregano)
1/8 teaspoon pepper
1 Tablespoon bread crumbs
1 Tablespoon grated Parmesan cheese
1/2 teaspoon garlic powder

Place halibut steaks in baking dish. Drizzle with wine and olive oil. Sprinkle with oregano, pepper, bread crumbs, Parmesan cheese, garlic powder and onion powder. Cover with wax paper. Cook on HIGH for 4-6 minutes, rearranging after half the time.

Rolled Fish Fillets Cradled in Spinach

1 clove minced garlic
2 Tablespoons olive oil
1 pound spinach, stems removed, washed, drained, cut
  into 1-inch strips
1/2 teaspoon lemon-pepper seasoning
4 thin white fish fillets (approximately 1 pound)
paprika to garnish

Place first 4 ingredients in a large casserole dish. Toss well.
Cover with plastic wrap and microwave on HIGH for 2 minutes.
Transfer spinach to a microwaveable platter, creating 4 piles and
leaving center open.

Loosely roll fish fillets, leaving space in center, and tucking
thinner end of fillet under thicker. Place fish, seam side down, on
spinach mounds. Sprinkle with paprika. Cover with wax paper
and microwave on HIGH for 7-9 minutes until fish flakes easily
with fork.

Salmon Steaks with Cucumbers and Capers

serves 2

2 (6-ounce) Salmon steaks, 3/4-inch thick
2 Tablespoons white wine
1/8 teaspoon black pepper
1/2 cup thinly sliced cucumber
1/2 cup pitted olives
3 Tablespoons chopped green onion
1 Tablespoon capers for garnish, rinsed and drained

Place salmon steaks in a shallow dish. Sprinkle with wine and
pepper and cover with wax paper. Microwave on MEDIUM
(50% power for 4 minutes. Rearrange and turn over. Re-cover
with wax paper and microwave an additional 3-5 minutes until
salmon is cooked through.

Remove steaks from dish and cover with foil to keep warm. Add cucumber, olives and green onions to the cooking liquid in the dish. Stir, cover with wax paper and microwave on HIGH for 1-2 minutes until warm. Spoon vegetables over salmon and garnish with capers.

Vegetable, Red Potato, and Fish Dinner

> 4 medium red thin-skinned potatoes
> 1/4 cup water
> 2 teaspoons olive oil
> 2 teaspoons margarine
> 1 medium onion, sliced into thin rings
> 1 clove garlic, minced
> 1 large bell pepper, sliced into rings
> 2 yellow crookneck squash, sliced into thin rounds
> 1 teaspoon salt-free seasoning
> 1 1/2 pounds white fish fillet, cut into 4 serving pieces
> 1 teaspoon paprika

Place potatoes and water in a 1 1/2-quart casserole dish. Cover and microwave on HIGH for 6-8 minutes until tender. Let stand until serving time.

In a glass pie plate combine oil, margarine, onion and garlic. Cover with plastic wrap and microwave on HIGH for 1 minute to melt margarine. Add bell pepper, squash and seasoning. Re-cover with plastic wrap and cook on HIGH for 4-5 minutes until vegetables are tender-crisp, stirring twice.

Arrange fish fillets on top of vegetables near edge of dish, with any thicker portions of fish to the outside. Re-cover and microwave on MEDIUM (50% power) for 8-12 minutes, until fish flakes easily with a fork, turning fish over halfway through cooking time.

To serve, divide vegetables among 4 soup plates, top with fish, sprinkle with paprika and add one potato to each bowl.

Crab Cakes

a taste of New England, better than fried

> 1/4 cup bread crumbs
> 1/2 teaspoon paprika
> 2 teaspoons parsley flakes
> 1 1/2 Tablespoons margarine
> 1 pound cooked crab meat, cartilage removed (or
>   imitation crab meat) picked into small pieces.
> 1/4 cup liquid egg substitute, beaten
> 1/4 cup mayonnaise or low-fat mayonnaise substitute
> 1 Tablespoon lemon juice
> 1 Tablespoon sherry
> 1/8 cup diced onion
> 1 clove garlic, minced
> 1/8 cup minced red bell pepper
> 1/2 teaspoon Dijon-style mustard

Place margarine in a glass pie plate and microwave on HIGH for 30-40 seconds to melt. Sprinkle in bread crumbs, paprika and parsley. Stir well to coat and spread in an even layer. Microwave on HIGH for 2 1/2-3 minutes until toasted, stirring once. Set aside.

In a large bowl, combine remaining ingredients, stirring well. Form 4 equal-size patties, 3/4-inch thick. Arrange in ring around outside of plate. Sprinkle with 1/4 of the bread crumbs, cover with a paper towel and microwave on HIGH for 7-9 minutes until heated through.

Seafood Chili

> 1 Tablespoon olive oil
> 1 large onion, chopped
> 1 clove garlic, chopped
> 1 Tablespoon chili powder
> 1/4 teaspoon ground cumin
> 1/4 teaspoon cayenne pepper
> 1/2 teaspoon dried oregano
> 1 (16-ounce) can stewed tomatoes
> 1 (16-ounce) can Great Northern beans, drained
> 1 medium bell pepper, chopped
> 1 pound shark, bones removed, cut to 1/2-inch cubes
> 2 Tablespoons fat-free plain yogurt, for garnish

Combine olive oil, onion and garlic in 2 1/2-quart casserole dish. Cover with wax paper and microwave on HIGH for 3 minutes until onion is tender-crisp. Stir in remaining ingredients except shark. Cover with wax paper and cook on HIGH for 5-6 minutes until boiling, stirring once

Place shark cubes in casserole around outer edges. Cover with wax paper and cook on MEDIUM (50% power) for 6-8 minutes until shark flakes easily. Spoon into bowls and garnish with a dollop of yogurt.

Shrimp in Wine

> 1 1/2 pounds medium size shrimp, washed, unpeeled
> 1 cup dry white wine
> 4 cloves garlic, minced
> 1 Tablespoon lemon juice
> 1 teaspoon Worcestershire sauce
> 1/4 teaspoon tarragon
> 1/4 teaspoon thyme
> 1/4 cup fresh chopped parsley for garnish

Combine all ingredients except parsley in a round 2 1/2 quart casserole dish. Arrange shrimp around the edge of the dish, leaving center open. Cover and cook on HIGH for 5-8 minutes until shrimp are pink and test done, stirring after half the cooking time..

To serve, divide shrimp and juice among 4 bowls and sprinkle with parsley.

Warm Moist Finger Towels

Just what's needed after eating Shrimp in Wine.

Combine 2 cups of water with 1 Tablespoon lime juice. Plunge 4 washcloths in water and wring out. Roll washcloths and cover with plastic wrap to keep moist until ready to use.

Before using, microwave covered washcloths for 1-2 minutes to warm, remove plastic, and place in bowl or basket.

POULTRY

Southwestern Chicken Bake

　　1/2 cup chopped onion
　　2 cloves minced garlic
　　1 teaspoon dried basil
　　1/2 teaspoon dried oregano
　　1 (8-ounce) can tomato sauce
　　1/2 cup water
　　1/4 cup dry wine
　　3 Tablespoons all-purpose flour
　　1/2 teaspoon ground cumin
　　1/2 teaspoon chili powder
　　4 boneless chicken breast halves, skinned

Combine onion, garlic, oregano and basil in a casserole dish and cook on HIGH for 1 minute. Add tomato sauce, water and wine, and stir. Cover and microwave on HIGH for 3 minutes. Let stand.

Combine flour and seasonings in a plastic bag. Drop chicken in bag and shake. Arrange coated chicken in a baking dish, thickest portions to the outside. Pour tomato sauce mixture over chicken and cover with wax paper. Cook on HIGH for 5 minutes. Reduce heat to MEDIUM LOW (30% power) for 10-15 minutes until chicken tests done.

Oriental Turkey and Sesame Seeds

　　4 medium carrots, chopped
　　1 1/2 cups instant brown rice
　　1 1/4 cups water
　　1 teaspoon soy sauce
　　1 teaspoon chicken bouillon
　　1 teaspoon honey
　　1 pound smoked cooked turkey, chopped
　　1 Tablespoon sesame seeds

In medium bowl cover and cook carrots on HIGH for 4 minutes until tender-crisp. Add water, rice, soy sauce, bouillon and honey. Cover and cook on HIGH for 8-10 minutes until rice is done. Stir in turkey and sesame seeds. Cover and cook on HIGH 2-3 minutes to heat throughout. Let stand 5 minutes.

Chicken with Mushroom Sauce

    1 Tablespoon margarine
    2 Tablespoons all-purpose flour
    2 Tablespoons white wine
    1/2 teaspoon dried basil
    1/4 teaspoon dried mustard
    1/4 teaspoon water
    1/2 cup water
    1/2 cup plain low-fat yogurt
    1 teaspoon low-salt chicken bouillon granules
    1/4 cup finely chopped green onions
    8 ounces fresh sliced mushrooms
    4 chicken breast halves, skin removed

Place margarine in medium bowl. Microwave on HIGH for 30 seconds or until melted. Add remaining ingredients, except chicken, mix well. Set aside.

Arrange chicken in baking dish with thickest portions to the outside. Cover and cook on HIGH for 7 minutes, rearranging after half the time. Discard grease. Pour mushroom sauce over chicken. Cover and reduce setting to MEDIUM (50% power) and cook for 6-10 minutes until sauce thickens slightly and chicken is done, stirring every 2 minutes to ensure even thickening.

Turkey Breast Half

Remove skin from turkey. Rinse and pat dry. Place turkey, meaty side down, in a baking dish. Cover and cook on MEDIUM (50% power) for 10-12 minutes per pound, turning over halfway through cooking time. (Turkey is done when meat is opaque, when juices run clear, and when an internal cooking temperature of 170-175 degrees Farenheit has been reached)

This produces a very juicy turkey breast and is an easy way to pre-cook meat for recipes that call for cooked turkey or chicken.

Browned Garlic Chicken

4 chicken pieces, skin and fat removed
1 teaspoon water
2 teaspoons Kitchen Bouquet browning sauce
1 egg white
2 cloves garlic, minced
1/2 cup onion, diced
freshly ground pepper to taste

In a small bowl whisk together coating ingredients. Brush on chicken. Place chicken in baking dish, meatiest portions to the outside. Cover and cook 6-7 minutes per pound, rearranging chicken twice. (Chicken is done when meat is opaque, when juices run clear, and when an internal temperature of 180-185 degrees Farenheit has been reached) Let stand 10 minutes.

New Potato Chicken Dinner

A hearty, delicious meal in a dish.

1 broiler-fryer cut up, skin and fat removed
1/4 teaspoon black pepper
1 teaspoon parsley flakes
1 large onion, sliced and rings separated
2 medium new potatoes, cubed
2 large carrots, sliced
1/2 cup frozen green beans, thawed
2 Tablespoons water

Arrange chicken in a large baking dish, thickest portions to the outside. Sprinkle with seasonings. Layer vegetables over chicken and sprinkle with water. Cover and microwave on MEDIUM HIGH (70% power) for 20-25 minutes, until chicken tests done, stirring twice and rearranging chicken once. (Remove cover carefully, avoiding steam.)

Herb Grilled Cornish Game Hens

In this recipe, hens are cooked in the microwave and then barbecue grilled to crisp and give extra flavor.

2 Cornish game hens (1 1/2 pound each) split lengthwise
2 Tablespoons olive oil
1/2 teaspoon dried parsley
1/2 teaspoon dried sage
1/4 teaspoon dried rosemary
1/4 teaspoon dried thyme

Preheat barbecue grill. Arrange hens breast side up, edges not touching in a 9 x 12-inch rectangular baking dish. Cover with wax paper and microwave on HIGH for 8 minutes. Rearrange hens and turn over. Cover again and microwave on HIGH for 8 minutes.

Combine oil and herbs in a small bowl. Place hens, skin side up on the grill and baste with the oil-herb mixture. Cook approximately 4 minutes. Turn hens over and cook an additional 4 minutes until browned.

Chicken and Rice with Vegetables

1 1/2 cups instant brown rice
2/3 cup water
1 teaspoon low-salt chicken bouillon granules
1 medium tomato, chopped
1/2 cup celery, chopped
1/2 cup zucchini, chopped
1 medium onion, chopped
1 clove garlic, minced
1/8-1/4 teaspoon black pepper
3 boneless chicken breast halves, without skin, cut into
 1-inch pieces

Combine all ingredients in baking dish. Cover. Microwave on HIGH for 8-10 minutes until chicken is done and liquid is absorbed. Stir once or twice.

Peachy Chicken

> 1 cup fresh, ripe, skinned peaches, chopped and
>   slightly crushed
> 1 teaspoon sugar or honey
> 1 teaspoon lemon juice
> 2 teaspoons cornstarch
> 4 chicken breast halves (or other pieces) skin removed
> pepper to taste
> 4 slices lemon
> fresh snipped parsley

In small bowl combine peaches and honey. Stir in cornstarch and lemon juice. Microwave on HIGH for 1 1/2- 2 1/2 minutes, or until mixture thickens, stirring once or twice. Microwave chicken on HIGH for 6-10 minutes or until test done. Pour sauce over chicken. Garnish with lemon and parsley.

Teriyaki Chicken

> Assorted chicken pieces (1 1/2 pounds), skin and fat
>   removed
>
> Sauce
> 1/4 cup Teriyaki sauce
> 1 Tablespoon lemon juice
> 1/4 teaspoon ground ginger
> 1 teaspoon sesame seeds

In a small bowl mix together sauce ingredients. Brush on chicken. Arrange chicken in a baking dish, meatiest portions to the outside. Cover and cook for 9-12 minutes on HIGH until meat tests done, rearranging and basting once. Let stand 10 minutes.

Eggplant Romano

The eggplant cooks deliciously in this recipe.

> 1/2 pound ground turkey
> 1 cup chopped onion
> 1/4 cup diced bell pepper
> 1/2 teaspoon dried oregano
> 1 teaspoon dried parsley
> dash cayenne pepper
> 1 medium eggplant, sliced into 1/4 inch rounds (peeling optional)
> 1 Tablespoon olive oil
> 1 (15-ounce) jar spaghetti sauce
> 2 Tablespoons wine
> 2 Tablespoons Parmesan cheese
> 4 cups hot cooked pasta or rice

Mix first 6 ingredients together in a microwaveable colander and place colander in a bowl. Microwave on HIGH for 4-5 minutes until turkey is no longer pink, stirring twice to break meat apart.

Arrange eggplant slices in 3-quart casserole dish. Drizzle with olive oil. Cover and cook on HIGH for 5 minutes or until tender. Pour spaghetti sauce, cooked turkey mixture and wine into a bowl and stir. Pour meat and sauce over eggplant. Cover. Cook on HIGH for 8-10 minutes until hot and bubbly. Sprinkle with Romano cheese. Serve over hot pasta or rice.

Parmesan Breaded Chicken

> Assorted chicken pieces (1 1/2 pounds), skin and fat
>   removed
> 1/2 teaspoon parsley flakes
> 1 Tablespoon Parmesan cheese
> 1/4 cup bread crumbs

Rinse chicken but do not pat dry. Sprinkle chicken with parsley, cheese and bread crumbs. Arrange in a baking dish with the meatiest portions to the outside. Cover loosely with wax paper and cook on HIGH for 9-12 minutes until chicken tests done, rearranging once. Let stand 10 minutes.

Broccoli and Ricotta Stuffed Chicken

> 2 teaspoons water
> 1/2 pound broccoli, coarsely chopped
> 1/3 cup part skim ricotta cheese
> 1/4 teaspoon garlic powder
> 1/4 teaspoon dried rosemary
> 1/2 teaspoon salt-free seasoning
> 2 whole boneless chicken breasts, halved, skinned,
>   pounded to flatten
> 2 teaspoons grated Parmesan cheese
> 1/4 teaspoon paprika

Place broccoli in a 1 1/2-quart casserole dish and sprinkle with water. Cover and cook on HIGH for 2-3 minutes until tender. Drain. Place ricotta in the container of a blender; puree. Blend in garlic powder, rosemary, seasoning and cooked broccoli.

Spoon mixture into center of each chicken piece. Roll up and place seam side down in a baking dish. Sprinkle with cheese and paprika. Cook on MEDIUM (50% power) for 6-8 minutes until chicken tests done. Cut each roll in half and serve.

Chicken Cacciatore

> 1 (7-ounce) package vermicelli
> 1 (15 1/2-ounce) can whole tomatoes, cut up
> 8 ounces fresh mushrooms, sliced
> 1 medium onion, sliced into rings
> 1/4 cup dry white wine
> 1 Tablespoon tomato paste
> 1/4 teaspoon dried oregano
> 1 teaspoon dried basil
> 4 skinned chicken breast halves
> 2 Tablespoons grated Romano cheese

Cook vermicelli according to package instructions on conventional stove top. Meanwhile, combine tomatoes with juice, mushrooms, onions, wine, tomato paste, and seasonings in a 2-quart casserole dish. Cover and cook on HIGH for 5-6 minutes until onions are tender.

Arrange chicken in a 12 x 8-inch baking dish with thickest portions to the outside. Pour vegetable sauce over chicken and cover with wax paper. Microwave on HIGH for 8-10 minutes until chicken tests done, rearranging and spooning sauce over chicken once. Serve chicken and sauce over pasta.

Chicken with Mushrooms and Artichoke Hearts

> 4 skinned chicken breast halves
> 8 ounces fresh mushrooms, sliced
> 1 (6-ounce) can artichoke hearts, drained, halved
> 1 teaspoon salt-free seasoning
> 1 (15-ounce) can low-salt whole tomatoes with juice, chopped
> 1 Tablespoon tomato paste

Arrange chicken in baking dish with pieces not touching and thickest portions to the outside. Spread mushrooms and artichoke hearts over chicken. Mix tomato paste and seasonings into tomatoes and pour over chicken. Cover and cook on MEDIUM HIGH (70% power) for 20-25 minutes until chicken tests done, rearranging and basting twice.

Lemon Chicken with Cauliflower

> 2 cups cauliflower florets
> 2 cups frozen green beans
> 1 medium onion, sliced
> 1 Tablespoon fresh lemon juice
> 3 Tablespoons white wine
> 1/4 teaspoon celery seed
> 1 teaspoon parsley flakes
> 4 boneless, skinless chicken breast halves
> 12 thin lemon slices

Combine all ingredients except chicken and lemon slices in a 3-quart casserole dish. Cover and cook on HIGH for 6-9 minutes or until vegetables are tender-crisp, stirring twice.

Place chicken in casserole dish, thickest portions to the outside, spooning vegetables over and around chicken. Cover everything with a layer of lemon slices. Cover with wax paper and cook on HIGH for 12-16 minutes until chicken tests done. Rearrange chicken pieces halfway through cooking time.

Turkey and Squash Casserole

> 1 cup yellow or crookneck squash, sliced into coins,
> larger sections quartered
> 1 cup sliced fresh mushrooms
> 1 medium onion, chopped
> 1 large stalk celery, chopped
> 2 slices whole wheat bread, toasted and cubed
> 1 Tablespoon minced fresh parsley or 1 teaspoon dried
> 2 cups cooked turkey, chopped
> 1/4 cup liquid egg substitute, or 2 egg whites, beaten
> 1 teaspoon salt-free seasoning
> 1 1/2 cups low-salt chicken broth
> 2 Tablespoons all-purpose flour

Place squash, mushrooms, onion and celery in a 2 1/2-quart casserole dish. Cover and cook on HIGH for 6-8 minutes until vegetables are tender-crisp, stirring once. Add bread, parsley, thyme, sage, turkey, egg substitute, and salt-free seasoning. Stir well.

In a small bowl, whisk together flour and broth until flour is completely dissolved. Microwave on HIGH for 3-4 minutes until thickened, whisking each 1 minute. Pour over chicken mixture and stir well. Cover and cook on HIGH for 8 minutes until hot and bubbly.

Easy Mexican Chicken Cutlets

> **1/2 cup whole wheat baking mix or bread crumbs**
> **2 teaspoons taco seasoning**
> **4 skinned, boned, chicken breast halves, rinsed but not dried**

Combine baking mix and taco seasoning on a plate. Roll chicken into mixture to coat. Arrange coated chicken in a 12 x 8-inch baking dish, edges of chicken not touching, largest portions to the outside. Cover with wax paper and microwave on HIGH for 5-7 minutes until chicken tests done.

Turkey Bacon

80 percent less fat than regular bacon.

> **4 slices turkey bacon**

Place turkey bacon on plate lined with paper towel and cover with another paper towel. Microwave on HIGH for 2 1/2-3 minutes to desired crispness.

Turkey Enchiladas

2 1/2 cups cooked turkey, cubed
3/4 cup low-fat ricotta cheese
1/4 cup diced green onion
1 teaspoon salt-free seasoning
8 (6-inch) tortillas, softened

Sauce
1 1/2 cups mild fresh salsa
1/2 teaspoon ground cumin
2 Tablespoons tomato paste

1/4 cup low-fat Cheddar cheese , shredded

Combine turkey, ricotta and onion in a medium bowl. Soften tortillas by wrapping in slightly damp paper towel and microwaving on HIGH for 1 minute. Spoon 1/8 of filling into center of each tortilla and roll up. Place seam side down in a baking dish.

Stir together sauce ingredients and pour over enchiladas. Cover with wax paper and cook on HIGH for 6-10 minutes until heated through, rotating dish after 4 minutes. Top with cheese and microwave on MEDIUM (50% power) for 1 minute to melt.

Ginger Chicken Stew

3 chicken breast halves, skin and fat removed
3 cups chopped celery
2 cups chopped carrots
2 cups chopped bell pepper
1 1/2 cups chopped onion
2 Tablespoons sesame seeds

Marinade
1/2 cup Teriyaki sauce
1 teaspoon lemon juice
1/2 teaspoon ground ginger

In a small bowl combine Teriyaki sauce, lemon juice and ginger. Place marinade ingredients and chicken in plastic bag. Refrigerate 1/2 hour, turning once.

Place chicken in a 12 x 8-inch baking dish. Set remaining marinade aside. Cook chicken on HIGH for 10-12 minutes until test done. Remove chicken and allow to cool. In same pan, add vegetables, sesame seeds and remaining marinade. Cover and cook on HIGH for 8-12 minutes until tender-crisp, stirring once.

While vegetables are cooking, chop chicken into bite-size pieces. Add chicken to vegetables and cook an additional 2-3 minutes on HIGH to heat throughout.

Chicken, Corn and White Bean Chili

serves 6

> 1 stalk celery, chopped
> 1 red bell pepper, diced
> 1 jalapeño pepper, seeded and minced
> 1 large onion, diced
> 2 cloves garlic, minced
> 1 3/4 cups water, divided
> 1 teaspoon chicken bouillon granules
> 1 cup frozen corn
> 1 cup frozen peas
> 1 teaspoon cumin
> 2 teaspoons chili powder
> 1/4 teaspoon black pepper
> 1 (16-ounce) can white beans
> 1 pound cooked chicken, chopped into 1-inch pieces

In a 3-quart casserole dish, combine celery, red pepper, jalapeño pepper, onion, garlic and 1/4 cup water. Cover and cook on HIGH for 4-6 minutes until vegetables are tender. Add remainder of water, bouillon granules, frozen corn and peas, and seasonings. Cover and cook on HIGH for 8-10 minutes, stirring twice. Stir in beans and chicken. Cover. Microwave on HIGH for 4 minutes. Reduce power and microwave on MEDIUM-LOW (50% power) for 15 minutes to blend flavors.

Spicy Black Bean Chili with Chicken

1 Tablespoon vegetable oil
1 clove garlic, minced
1 medium onion, chopped
2 stalks celery, sliced
1 pound boneless chicken cutlets cut into 1-inch cubes
2 Tablespoons all-purpose flour
1 (14-ounce) can black beans, drained
2 cups low-salt chicken broth
1-2 serrano or jalapeño chili peppers (depending on
    hotness desired), chopped
1/2 teaspoon dried thyme
1 teaspoon ground cumin
1/8 teaspoon salt
1/8 teaspoon black pepper

In a 2-quart casserole dish combine oil, garlic, onion and celery.
Cover and microwave on HIGH for 3-4 minutes until onion is
tender. Add the chicken and sprinkle with flour. Stir. Cover and
cook on HIGH for 4-5 minutes, stirring once to move center
pieces to the outside. Stir in remaining ingredients. Cover and
cook on HIGH for 6-7 minutes until chicken is tender and flavors
have blended, stirring once during cooking time.

Chicken Barbecue Drumsticks

1/4 cup chopped onion
2 Tablespoons chopped celery
1 teaspoon Dijon mustard
1 teaspoon Worcestershire sauce
1/8 teaspoon pepper
3/4 cup barbecue sauce
8 skinless chicken drumsticks

Mix all ingredients except chicken in a small bowl. Set sauce aside. Place chicken in shallow baking dish with pieces not touching and thickest portions to the outside. Brush with 1/3 of the sauce. Cover and cook on HIGH for 5 minutes. Turn and rearrange chicken. Brush with another 1/3 of the sauce. Cover and cook on HIGH for 5 minutes. Rearrange chicken. Brush with remaining sauce. Cover loosely and cook for 1-5 minutes until chicken is done and sauce is hot.

Lemon Marinated Grape Chicken

        1/3 cup lemon juice
        1/2 cup water
        1 teaspoon Worcestershire sauce
        1/4 teaspoon garlic powder
        1/8 teaspoon pepper
        4 chicken breast halves, skin removed
        1/4 pound seedless green grapes, sliced in half along
            length
        fresh snipped parsley for garnish

In a 2-cup microwaveable measure mix together first 5 ingredients to make marinade. Microwave on HIGH for 1 to 2 minutes. Pour in plastic bag. Add chicken. Refrigerate for 1-2 hours.

Place chicken in 2 quart baking dish, thickest portions to the outside, pieces not touching. Drizzle 1-2 Tablespoons of marinade over chicken and cover. Microwave on HIGH for 10-12 minutes or until done, rearranging and basting with 1-2 Tablespoons of marinade twice, and adding grapes for last 2 minutes of cooking time.

Garnish with parsley and serve.

Curry Chicken with Dates

       1 1/2 cups chicken broth
       1 Tablespoon sunflower oil
       1 cup chopped onion
       1 clove garlic
       1 cup frozen peas
       1 Tablespoon curry powder
       1/8 cup all-purpose flour
       1 pound boneless chicken breasts cut into 1-inch cubes
       1/8 cup plus 4 Tablespoons pitted, chopped dates
       4-6 cups hot cooked rice

Cook rice on conventional stove top according to package directions. Meanwhile, pour broth into a small bowl and heat on HIGH for 3 minutes. Set aside. (This will reduce cooking time later.)

In a 3-quart casserole dish, combine oil, onion, garlic and peas. Cover and microwave on HIGH for 3-4 minutes until tender-crisp, stirring once. Sprinkle flour over vegetables and blend. Slowly pour broth over vegetables and stir. Cover and microwave on HIGH for 4-5 minutes until beginning to boil and thicken, stirring twice.

Add chicken and dates. Stir well and re-cover, cooking on HIGH for 5-7 minutes until chicken is done, stirring once. Let stand 5 minutes.

Serve over hot rice and garnish with remaining dates.

Turkey with Green Chili and Tortilla Chips

serves 6

> 1 teaspoon olive oil
> 1/3 cup chopped red or green bell pepper
> 1/2 cup chopped onion
> 1 clove chopped garlic
> 1 stalk celery, chopped
> 1/8 teaspoon cumin
> 1 cup boiling water
> 2 teaspoons low-salt beef bouillon granules
> 3 Tablespoons flour
> 1/4 cup plus 2 Tablespoons canned, chopped green
>   chiles
> 2 egg whites
> 1 cup plain nonfat yogurt
> 2 cups chopped, cooked turkey
> 4-5 cups baked, low-salt tortilla chips
> 1/2 cup sliced ripe olives
> 1/4 cup chopped green onion
> 1 small tomato diced

In a large baking dish mix olive oil, bell pepper, onion, garlic and cumin. Cover. Cook on HIGH for 2 minutes to soften vegetables.

Into 1 cup boiling water dissolve the beef bouillon granules. Pour over vegetables. Sprinkle flour over vegetables, add chiles, and stir well. Cover and microwave on HIGH for 2 1/2-3 minutes, stirring once to ensure even thickening.

In medium bowl beat egg whites. Transfer the yogurt, chicken and vegetable mixture to the bowl with the egg whites. Mix well.

Pour the tortilla chips into bottom of the baking dish. Press with hands to slightly break and form an even layer. Pour chicken sauce over chips, completely covering. Cover and cook on MEDIUM HIGH (70% power) for 10-12 minutes, repositioning dish in oven halfway through cooking time. Keep chips covered with sauce. To serve, garnish with olives, green onion, tomato and the remaining chiles.

Turkey Stroganoff

Also use the meatballs as appetizers, in soup, or with spaghetti sauce. They freeze well.

>**Meatballs**
>1/2 cup bread crumbs
>1 Tablespoon parsley flakes
>1/4 teaspoon pepper
>1/4 cup onion, chopped small
>2 egg whites, slightly beaten
>1 pound ground turkey
>
>**Sauce**
>2 cups fresh sliced mushrooms
>1/4 cup diced green onion
>1 1/2 cups skim milk
>1/2 cup plain nonfat yogurt
>4 Tablespoons all-purpose flour
>1/4 cup white wine
>
>4 cups hot cooked rice or noodles

Cook rice or noodles according to package directions on conventional stove top. Meanwhile, combine bread crumbs, parsley, pepper, onion, and egg whites in a medium bowl. Add turkey and mix well. Shape into about 40 1-inch balls. Place in a baking dish and cook uncovered on HIGH for 5-7 minutes, or until done, rearranging after half the time. Set aside.

In medium bowl whisk together milk, yogurt, flour and wine. Add mushrooms. Cover and microwave on HIGH for 4-6 minutes stirring every 1 1/2 minutes to ensure even thickening. Add sauce to meatballs, stirring and coating with sauce. Cover. Cook on HIGH for 5-7 minutes, until hot throughout, stirring twice. Serve over long-grain rice or noodles.

Turkey Chili with Black Beans

1 medium onion, chopped
1 pound ground turkey
1 bell pepper, diced
1 (28-ounce) can crushed tomatoes
1 (15-ounce) can black beans, rinsed or 1 1/2 cups
   cooked black beans
4 ounces fresh sliced mushrooms
2 teaspoons chili powder
1 teaspoon ground cumin
1/4 teaspoon dried oregano
1/4 teaspoon black pepper

Combine onion, turkey and bell pepper in microwaveable colander. Place colander in bowl and microwave on HIGH for 5-6 minutes until turkey is no longer pink, stirring twice to break meat apart.

Place meat mixture in a 3-quart casserole dish and add remainder of ingredients. Cover with wax paper and microwave on HIGH for 5 minutes. Reduce heat to MEDIUM LOW (30% power) and simmer for 30 minutes.

Sliced New Potato Casserole with Bits of Tomato

1 (16-ounce) can low-salt stewed tomatoes
1/4 teaspoon black pepper
1/2 teaspoon dried basil
5 medium thin-skinned potatoes, sliced 1/8-inch thick
1 pound ground, turkey, crumbled into little pieces
3/4 cup grated low-fat Cheddar cheese

In a 3-quart baking dish, combine tomatoes, pepper, basil and potatoes. Cover and microwave on HIGH for 14-16 minutes, stirring twice. Stir in turkey, re-cover, and cook on HIGH for 8-12 minutes until meat is no longer pink, stirring gently, once.

Gently stir in 1/2 the cheese and top with the remaining half. Let stand 10 minutes to melt the cheese.

Chicken Italiano

serves 6

>   6-8 cups cooked rice or pasta
>   3 pounds fryer chicken, cut into parts, skin and fat
>   removed
>   1 (32-ounce) jar spaghetti sauce
>   1/2 pound sliced fresh mushrooms
>   1 large green bell pepper, sliced into thin 2-inch long
>   strips
>   1 medium tomato, coarsely chopped
>   1/4 cup white wine
>   2 Tablespoons grated Romano cheese, for garnish

Cook rice or pasta according to package directions on
conventional stove top. Meanwhile, arrange chicken in a deep 3-
quart casserole dish. Cover and microwave on HIGH for 15
minutes, rearranging twice. Discard grease. In a large bowl,
combine spaghetti sauce, mushrooms, bell pepper, tomato and
wine. Pour over chicken. Cover loosely and cook on HIGH for 7-
12 minutes until chicken is done and vegetables are tender,
stirring and rearranging once. Serve over rice or pasta. Garnish
with Romano cheese.

Spicy Chili

serves 8

>   1 pound lean ground turkey
>   1 green bell pepper, chopped
>   1 large onion, chopped
>   3 cloves garlic, minced
>   1 (4-ounce) can chopped green chilies drained
>   1 bay leaf
>   1 teaspoon cumin
>   1 Tablespoon chili powder
>   1 teaspoon paprika
>   1 teaspoon oregano
>   1 (28-ounce) can low-salt tomato sauce
>   2 (16-ounce) cans kidney beans

Place turkey in a microwaveable colander and place colander in bowl. Microwave on HIGH for 6-8 minutes until no longer pink, stirring twice to break apart.

In a 3-quart casserole dish, combine turkey, bell pepper, onion, garlic and chilies. Cover and microwave on HIGH for 4-5 minutes until vegetables are tender, stirring once.

Add remainder of ingredients. Mix well. Cover and microwave on HIGH for 10-12 minutes until beginning to boil. Reduce power and simmer on MEDIUM LOW (30% power) for 45 minutes to blend flavors.

Turkey Burgers

> 1 pound ground turkey
> 1/2 cup dry bread crumbs
> 1/2 teaspoon pepper
> 1 Tablespoon dried parsley
> 1/2 cup nonfat milk
> 1 teaspoon Worcestershire sauce
> 1/3 cup chopped onions

In medium bowl mix together all ingredients. Shape into four 1-inch thick patties. Place in shallow baking dish, edges not touching. Cover and cook on HIGH for 5-7 minutes, until test done.

Serve on whole wheat hamburger buns. Variations; try topping with avocado, cooked mushrooms, or low-fat cheese.

Taco Rice Supper

        1/2 pound ground turkey
        1/2 cup green onion, chopped
        1 Tablespoon fresh cilantro
        1 (8-ounce) can low-salt tomato sauce
        1/2 cup mild salsa
        1/2 teaspoon garlic powder
        1/8 teaspoon black pepper
        1 1/2 cups instant brown rice, cooked
        4 cups chopped lettuce
        3 small tomatoes, chopped
        2 ounces shredded fat-free Cheddar cheese, for garnish
        1/4 cup chopped ripe pitted olives, for garnish

Place turkey, onion and cilantro in microwaveable colander and place colander in a bowl. Microwave on HIGH for 3-5 minutes until meat is no longer pink, stirring twice to break apart.

Combine turkey and onion, with tomato sauce, salsa, garlic powder and pepper in a 2-quart casserole dish. Cover and microwave on HIGH for 4-5 minutes until mixture begins to boil. Stir in rice and let stand 5 minutes.

Line 4 plates with lettuce and tomatoes. Spoon 1/4 of the turkey-rice mixture onto each. Garnish with cheese and olives.

Sis's Green Bean Stew

        1 pound ground turkey
        3 cups boiling water
        2 cups green beans
        2 cups carrots, sliced into 1/8-inch thick rounds
        2 cups potatoes, peeled and chopped into 1/2-inch
            cubes
        2 teaspoons low-salt chicken bouillon granules
        1/2 teaspoon garlic powder
        1 teaspoon dried parsley
        pepper to taste

Crumble ground turkey in a microwaveable colander and place colander in a bowl. Microwave on HIGH for 5-7 minutes until no longer pink, stirring twice to break meat apart.

Pour one cup of boiling water into a 3-quart casserole dish. Add green beans and carrots. Cover and microwave on HIGH for 5 minutes. Add potatoes, re-cover and microwave on HIGH 5 more minutes.

Add remaining 2 cups boiling water, chicken bouillon, garlic and onion powder, parsley, pepper, and cooked ground turkey. Cover loosely and cook on HIGH for 5-10 minutes until vegetables are soft and flavors have blended.

Spaghetti with Ground Turkey

yields 8 cups

Traditional flavor without the saturated fat and cholesterol.

1 pound ground turkey
2 Tablespoons olive oil
4 cloves garlic, minced
1 large onion, finely chopped
1 medium green pepper, diced
1 (14-ounce) can low-salt crushed tomatoes
1 (15-ounce) can low-salt tomato sauce
2 Tablespoons tomato paste
2 teaspoons dried oregano
1 teaspoon dried basil
1/2 teaspoon paprika
1/2 cup fresh parsley, minced
dash cayenne pepper
dash salt
black pepper to taste
hot cooked spaghetti
1/4 cup grated Parmesan cheese for garnish

Cook spaghetti according to package directions on conventional stove top.

Meanwhile, crumble turkey into a microwaveable colander and place colander in a bowl. Microwave on HIGH for 6-8 minutes until no longer pink, stirring twice to break apart meat.

Combine turkey and remaining ingredients in a 3-quart casserole dish. Cover with wax paper and cook on HIGH for 10 minutes, then reduce power to MEDIUM LOW (30% power) for 30 to 40 minutes until sauce thickens to desired consistency, stirring occasionally.

Ladle sauce over hot cooked spaghetti, sprinkle with cheese, and serve.

MEATS

Lamb Chops with New Potatoes

6 small new potatoes, quartered
1 cup sliced celery
1/2 teaspoon dried thyme
8 (4-ounce) lamb loin chops, 1-inch thick
1 onion, sliced into rings
1/2 teaspoon lemon-pepper seasoning
1/4 teaspoon garlic powder

In each of 4 individual 2-cup casserole dishes, layer 1/4 of potato quarters, celery, and thyme.

Trim all fat from chops and place 2 atop each vegetable mixture in dishes. Cover with onion rings and sprinkle with lemon-pepper seasoning. Cover and cook on HIGH for 10 minutes. Give dishes a half turn and rearrange after half the cooking time.

Reduce power to MEDIUM LOW (30% power) and cook for 20-25 minutes until meat and vegetables are tender, half turning dishes once. Spoon juices over meat and vegetables.

Oriental Beef Stew

1 pound boneless beef chuck roast, trimmed of fat,
    pierced all over with a fork, cut into 1/2-inch cubes
1/2 teaspoon ground ginger
2 teaspoons low-salt beef bouillon granules
2 cups hot water
1/4 cup lite Teriyaki sauce
1 large onion, sliced into rings
1 small red bell pepper, cut into strips
2 cups fresh bean sprouts
1 (10-ounce) package frozen snow peas
1 cup sliced mushrooms

Place meat in a 3-quart casserole dish. Dissolve bouillon granules into hot water and stir in ginger and Teriyaki sauce. Pour over meat. Add onions. Cover and cook on HIGH for 10 minutes, stirring twice, keeping meat covered with liquid.

Reduce heat to MEDIUM LOW (30% power) and cook for 40-50 minutes, stirring twice.

When meat is tender and no longer pink, add bell pepper, sprouts and snow peas, covering them with meat and juice. Cover and microwave on MEDIUM LOW for 10-12 minutes until vegetables are tender-crisp. Skim off fat and serve.

Meatball Casserole

> 1 pound extra lean ground beef
> 1 small minced onion
> 1/4 cup quick-cooking oats
> 1/4 cup skim milk
> 1 teaspoon dried basil
> 1/8 teaspoon black pepper
> 1 medium zucchini, chopped
> 2 small yellow crookneck squash, chopped
> 1 cup frozen green beans
> 2 Tablespoons water
> 1 cup low-salt tomato sauce
> 1 teaspoon chili powder

Mix together beef, onion, oats, milk, basil and pepper in a medium bowl. Form into 8 meatballs. Place in a 12 x 7-inch baking dish. Cover and microwave on HIGH for 6 minutes until meat is no longer pink, rearranging once. Drain.

In a 2-quart casserole dish, combine zucchini, squash, frozen beans and water. Cover and microwave on HIGH for 6-8 minutes, until tender, stirring once.

Gently stir in tomato sauce, chili powder, and meatballs. Cover and microwave on HIGH for 3-5 minutes.

Italian Stuffed Peppers

1 cup cooked instant brown rice
8 ounces extra lean ground beef
1 small chopped zucchini
6 medium fresh mushrooms, sliced
1 small chopped onion
1 cup chopped seeded tomatoes
1/2 teaspoon dried oregano
2 large green bell peppers, halved lengthwise
3 Tablespoons chopped black olives
1/4 cup plain low-fat yogurt
dash paprika

Cook rice according to package directions on conventional stove top. Meanwhile, crumble meat in a microwaveable colander and place colander in a bowl. Stir in zucchini and onions. Cook on HIGH for 3-4 minutes until meat is no longer pink. Transfer meat-vegetable mixture to a medium bowl and stir in rice, tomatoes and oregano. Set aside. Place bell peppers, cut-side-down, on a plate. Cover and microwave on HIGH for 3-5 minutes until tender, and drain.

Turn peppers cut-side-up and spoon meat mixture into peppers. Cover and microwave on HIGH for 5-7 minutes until heated through. Top with yogurt, black olives and paprika.

Simmered Round Steak

1 pound round steak, trimmed of fat, tenderized, cut into serving sized pieces
2 Tablespoons all-purpose flour
1 teaspoon salt-free seasoning
1/2 teaspoon garlic powder
1/4 teaspoon black pepper
1 medium onion, sliced into rings
1 stalk celery, sliced
1 cup hot water
1 teaspoon beef bouillon granules
1 teaspoon Worcestershire sauce

In a shallow dish, combine flour, salt-free seasoning, garlic powder and pepper. Roll meat in flour mixture. Place in baking dish and top with onion and celery.

Dissolve bouillon granules in hot water, add Worcestershire sauce and pour over steaks. Cover and microwave on HIGH for 5 minutes. Reduce power to MEDIUM (50% power) and cook for 20-25 minutes until fork-tender, rearranging steaks after half the cooking time.

Pineapple-Glazed Ham Slice

> 1 can (8-ounce) crushed pineapple with unsweetened juice
> 1 teaspoon cornstarch
> 1 teaspoon packed brown sugar
> 1 (1 pound) cooked lean ham slice, 1/2-inch thick

In a small bowl dissolve cornstarch with a small amount of the pineapple juice. Add remainder of the pineapple juice, pineapple chunks and sugar. Microwave on HIGH for 1-2 minutes. Set aside.

Place ham slice in a baking dish. Cover with wax paper and microwave on MEDIUM (50% power) for 5 minutes. Remove paper and spoon pineapple mixture on top. Microwave on MEDIUM another 2-3 minutes until heated through.

Easy Mexican Pork Chops

> 3 Tablespoons taco seasoning powder
> 1/2 cup breadcrumbs
> 4 pork chops, trimmed of fat

Pour seasoning powder and breadcrumbs into a plastic bag. Drop in one pork chop at a time and shake to coat. Arrange chops in a baking dish and cover with wax paper. Microwave on MEDIUM HIGH (70% power) for 10 minutes. Rearrange and turn over pork chops and continue to microwave on MEDIUM HIGH an additional 12-16 minutes until meat is done.

Veal Mozzarella

1 pound veal cutlets, pounded 1/4-inch thick
1 medium onion sliced into rings
3 Tablespoons hot water
3 Tablespoons dry white wine
1/4 cup tomato paste
1/2 teaspoon garlic powder
1/2 teaspoon dried basil
1/2 cup plain low-fat yogurt
1/2 cup shredded low-fat mozzarella cheese
1/4 cup chopped fresh parsley

In a 7 x 11-inch baking dish, place veal in a single layer on the bottom, and arrange onion on the top. Set aside.

In a 4-cup measure blend wine, water, tomato paste, garlic and basil. Microwave on HIGH for 2-3 minutes until thickened, stirring each 1 minute. Add yogurt, stir, and pour over veal. Cover and microwave on MEDIUM (50% power) for 10-14 minutes until veal is done, rearranging after half the cooking time. Sprinkle with mozzarella and parsley and microwave another 1 minute on MEDIUM to melt the cheese.

Beef and New Potato Dinner

10 ounces beef round steak, pierced all over, trimmed of fat, and cut into 1/2-inch cubes
1 large onion, sliced, rings separated
1 1/4 cups water
3/4 cup Burgundy wine
1 Tablespoon tomato paste
1 Tablespoon low-salt beef bouillon granules
2 medium new potatoes cubed
1 bay leaf
1/2 teaspoon thyme
1 large tomato, chopped
2 cups hot cooked noodles

Cook noodles according to package directions on conventional oven top. Meanwhile, in a 2 1/2-quart casserole, combine beef, onions, water, wine, tomato paste, beef bouillon, potatoes, bay leaf and thyme. Mix well making sure beef is covered by liquid. Cover and cook on HIGH for 10 minutes. Reduce heat to MEDIUM LOW (30% power). Re-cover and cook for 55-65 minutes until meat is done and vegetables are tender, stirring twice. Stir in chopped tomatoes and let stand 10 minutes. Serve over hot cooked noodles.

Rice and Veal

4 veal loin chops, 1/2-inch thick, trimmed of fat
2 green onions, chopped
1 cup instant brown rice
2 small yellow crookneck squash, chopped
1/2 teaspoon dried oregano
1/2 teaspoon dried basil
1 cup low-salt tomato juice
8 ounces fresh sliced mushrooms

In each of 4 individual 2-cup casserole dishes, place 1 veal chop. In small bowl, combine onion, rice, squash, oregano, basil, and juice. Spoon rice and vegetables around meat. Top with mushrooms. Cover and microwave on HIGH for 10 minutes, rotating dishes on half turn, half way through cooking time. Rearrange dishes and reduce power to MEDIUM LOW (30% power). Microwave for 20-25 minutes, turning dishes once.

Steak and Beans Olé

1 pound beef round steak, cut in 1-inch cubes
1/4 cup dry white wine
1/4 cup water
1 small onion
1 tomato, chopped
1 medium zucchini, diced
1 (10-ounce) package frozen corn
1 (4-ounce) can chopped green chile
1 clove garlic, diced
1/4 teaspoon dried oregano
1 (16-ounce) can pinto beans, drained

Place beef, water and wine in a 2 1/2-quart casserole dish and cover. Cook on MEDIUM (50% power) for 12 minutes. Stir in remaining ingredients and cook on MEDIUM HIGH (70% power) for 20-25 minutes until meat is tender, stirring twice.

Mini Vegetable Meat Loaves

1 pound extra lean ground beef
1 egg white
1 teaspoon Worcestershire sauce
1 small onion, chopped
1 carrot, grated
1 stalk of celery, chopped
2 teaspoons fresh minced parsley
2 cloves of garlic, minced
1/2 teaspoon dried basil
1/8 teaspoon nutmeg

Sauce
1 cup salt-free tomato sauce
1/4 teaspoon cayenne pepper
1/2 teaspoon dry mustard
1/4 teaspoon oregano
1 1/2 Tablespoons brown sugar

Combine ground beef and egg with vegetables and seasonings. Shape into 4 uniform sized mini-loaves. Arrange loaves in pie plate like spokes in a wagon wheel. Cover with wax paper and microwave on HIGH for 7-8 minutes until test done, rotating dish 1/2 turn after half the time.

Mix together all sauce ingredients and pour over loaves. Cook on HIGH for 2-3 minutes.

Green Chili and Corn with Pork

1 teaspoon vegetable oil
1 large onion, chopped
1 large clove garlic, minced
1 pound boneless pork, trimmed, cut into 1-inch cubes
2 Tablespoons all-purpose flour
2 (4-ounce) cans chopped mild green chilies, drained
2 cups frozen corn
1-2 serrano or jalapeño chili (depending on degree of
    hotness desired), chopped
1 1/2 cups chicken broth
1/2 teaspoon dried oregano
1/2 teaspoon ground cumin
1/4 teaspoon black pepper

In 3-quart casserole dish, combine oil, onion and garlic. Cover and microwave on HIGH for 2-3 minutes until onions are tender-crisp.

In a large bowl, toss pork with flour to coat. Add pork to onion mixture and stir. Cover and cook on HIGH for 8-12 minutes until no longer pink, stirring once to move center pieces to outside.

Stir in remaining ingredients. Cover and microwave on HIGH for 6-7 minutes until boiling. Reduce heat to MEDIUM LOW (30% power) and simmer for 20-30 minutes to blend flavors.

Lamb Steaks Marinated in Wine

> 4 lamb sirloin steaks, 1/2-inch thick, trimmed of fat
>   and pierced with fork all over
> 1 medium chopped onion
> 1/4 teaspoon dill weed
> 1/2 teaspoon dry mustard
> 1/4 cup dry white wine
> 2 Tablespoons lemon juice

Place steaks flat in a 12 x 8-inch baking dish. In a small bowl, combine onion, dill mustard, wine and lemon juice. Pour over steaks. Cover and refrigerate 8-12 hours, turning twice.

After marinating, keep covered, and microwave on HIGH for 5 minutes. Rearrange steaks and turn over. Reduce heat to MEDIUM LOW (30% power) and cook for 8-10 minutes until meat is tender and no longer pink. Skim fat from juices and spoon juices over lamb.

Elliot's Mushy Cushy Individual Bakes

> 2 small potatoes, sliced into 1/2-inch cubes
> 1 small onion, sliced into 1/2 -inch cubes
> 2 cups frozen peas
> 4 extra lean ground beef patties, 1/2-inch thick
> 1 medium tomato, diced
> 14 teaspoons garlic powder
> 14 teaspoons onion powder
> 1 Tablespoon Parmesan cheese

Into 4 individual 2 cup casserole dishes layer potatoes and onions. Cover and microwave on HIGH for 3 minutes

Next, layer peas, beef patty, and tomatoes atop potatoes and onions. Sprinkle with garlic, onion powder and Parmesan cheese. Cover and microwave on HIGH for 10 minutes, giving each casserole a half turn once.

Rearrange casseroles and reduce power to MEDIUM LOW (30% power). Microwave for 8-10 minutes until meat is done and vegetables are tender.

Veal Italiano

2 cups fresh mushroom slices
1/4 cup sliced green onion
1/3 cup red bell pepper, diced
1/4 cup dry white wine
1 teaspoon low-salt bouillon granules
1/4 teaspoon garlic powder
1/2 teaspoon lemon pepper seasoning
4 (4-ounce) veal cutlets

In a baking dish, combine all ingredients except lemon-pepper seasoning and veal. Cover and microwave on HIGH for 5 minutes until vegetables are tender, stirring once.

Sprinkle lemon-pepper on veal and arrange veal in the baking dish, spooning, mushroom mixture over top. Cover and microwave on HIGH for 5 minutes.

Rearrange meat, cover with mushroom mixture and cover dish. Cook an additional 7-10 minutes on MEDIUM-LOW (30% power) until veal is tender.

Meat Balls

1 pound extra lean ground beef
1/4 cup egg substitute, lightly beaten
1/2 cup grated carrot
1/8 teaspoon black pepper
1/2 teaspoon dried basil
1/4 teaspoon dried oregano
2 Tablespoons dry wine

Blend together all ingredients and form into about 36 1-inch meatballs. Arrange in 12 x 8-inch baking dish. Cover with wax paper and cook on HIGH for 6-10 minutes until meatballs are firm and no longer pink, rearranging after half the time. Drain.

Simmered Lamb Steaks

    4 (4-ounce) lamb leg steaks, trimmed of fat
    1 medium onion, chopped
    1 (8-ounce) can low-salt stewed tomatoes
    1 Tablespoon tomato paste
    3 Tablespoons dry white wine
    1/4 cup fresh chopped parsley

In a baking dish, arrange steaks with the thickest portion to the outside.

In a medium bowl, combine onion, tomatoes, tomato paste, wine and parsley. Pour over lamb. Cover and microwave on HIGH for 5 minutes.

Reduce power to MEDIUM LOW (30% power) and simmer for 30-35 minutes, rearranging steaks half way through cooking time. Cut to test for doneness.

SAUCES/DIPS/SPREADS

Avocado Dip

yields 1 1/2-2 cups

Great over steamed vegetables, potatoes, and as a dip, especially with steamed artichoke.

> **1 large ripe but not mushy avocado**
> **1/2 cup water**
> **2 Tablespoons lemon juice**
> **1/2 teaspoon salt-free seasoning**

Slice avocado in half, remove pit, and spoon flesh into blender. Add, remaining ingredients and puree.

Mayonnaise with Fresh Cilantro Dip

Delicious with steamed artichokes!

> **1 cup low-fat mayonnaise or Nayonaise (mayonnaise substitute)**
> **1 Tablespoon lime juice**
> **3/4 cup chopped fresh chopped cilantro**
> **1 teaspoon parsley flakes**

Combine all ingredients in a small bowl. Stir well and refrigerate until serving time.

Basil Parsley Dip

yields 1 1/2 cups

A wonderful butter substitute for fresh corn on the cob.

> **1 cup low-fat mayonnaise or Nayonaise (mayonnaise substitute)**
> **1 Tablespoon lemon juice**
> **1/2 cup fresh chopped parsley**
> **1/2 cup fresh chopped basil**

In a small bowl, combine all ingredients and refrigerate until serving time.

Tartar Sauce with Herbs and Parmesan Cheese

yields 1 cup

> 2/3 cup plain low-fat yogurt
> 1/3 cup low-fat mayonnaise or mayonnaise substitute
> 2 Tablespoons grated low-fat Parmesan cheese
> 1/2 teaspoon dried sage
> 1/2 teaspoon onion powder
> 1/4 teaspoon paprika

Combine all ingredients in a small bowl. Refrigerate 1/2 hour to blend flavors.

Corn Salsa

A great side dish with fish steaks.

> 2 medium tomatoes, chopped
> 1 cup frozen corn kernels, thawed
> 1 Tablespoon minced fresh cilantro
> 2 Tablespoons minced green onion
> 2 teaspoons olive oil
> 1/2 teaspoon fresh lime juice
> 1/2 teaspoon minced fresh jalapeño chili pepper

In a small bowl, mix together all ingredients and chill for 1 hour to allow flavors to blend.

Tri-Color Bell Pepper Dip

> 1 Tablespoon olive oil
> 1 medium red onion, thinly sliced, rings separated
> 1 large clove garlic, minced
> 3 small bell peppers (yellow, green and red) cut
>   into 1/4-inch pieces
> 1 teaspoon salt-free seasoning

Combine all ingredients in a 2-quart casserole dish. Cover and microwave on HIGH for 4-6 minutes until vegetables are tender, stirring once.

Guacamole with Turkey-Bacon

yields 2 cups

> 4 slices turkey bacon, chopped
> 2 ripe avocados
> 2 Tablespoons fresh lemon juice
> 1 medium tomato, seeded and chopped
> 1/4 cup finely minced onion
> 1/2-1 serrano chili pepper, finely chopped
> 1/4 teaspoon garlic powder
> 1/4 teaspoon dried oregano
> 1/4 teaspoon black pepper

Place turkey-bacon between two paper towels and microwave on HIGH for 3-4 minutes to desired crispness. Allow to cool.

In a small bowl, mash avocados. Stir in all ingredients.

Simple Salsa

> 2 medium tomatoes, chopped
> 1 medium onion, chopped
> 1/2-2 serrano chile peppers, minced
> 1 Tablespoon lemon juice
> 1 Tablespoon water
> 1 Tablespoon chopped cilantro
> 1/4 teaspoon garlic powder
> 1/4 teaspoon ground cumin

Blend all ingredients in a small bowl. Serve at room temperature or chilled.

Peach Sauce

yields 1 1/2 cups

Very versatile. Goes equally well over chicken, cake, or frozen yogurt.

1 cup fresh chopped peaches (or frozen chopped peaches thawed)
1 Tablespoon cornstarch
1 1/2 Tablespoons sugar
1/2 cup apple juice

In a 4-cup microwaveable measure, combine cornstarch, sugar and apple juice. Stir in peaches. Microwave on HIGH for 2 1/2-3 minutes until syrup is thickened, stirring each 1 minute during cocking.

Easy Pesto

>2 large cloves garlic
>4 cups fresh basil leaves (may substitute 4 cups fresh
>spinach leaves and 2 teaspoons dried basil)
>1/2 cup pine nuts (may substitute walnuts or almonds)
>1/2 cup extra-virgin olive oil

In food processor, mince garlic. Add basil leaves and chop finely, add pine nuts and chop finely. Drizzle in olive oil in a fine stream to form a thick paste.

Before serving, add 1/2 cup hot water to 1/4 cup Pesto, and stir well.

Pesto keeps for weeks refrigerated. Place in jar, cover with a layer of olive oil to prevent browning, and cover with a tight-fitting lid.

Pesto also freezes well. Freeze in an ice cube tray. Transfer cubes to plastic bag and tie shut.

Bright Teriyaki Sauce

Excellent over salad greens, cooked vegetables, chicken, and fish.

>1/4 cup Teriyaki sauce
>1 Tablespoon lemon
>1/4 teaspoon ground ginger

Combine all ingredients in a small bowl.

Tangy Barbecue Sauce

yields 2 cups

>1 teaspoon olive oil
>1 teaspoon margarine

1 large onion finely chopped
1 large clove garlic, minced
1 cup ketchup
1/4 cup cider vinegar
2 Tablespoons honey
2 Tablespoons soy sauce
2 Tablespoons Worcestershire sauce
1/2 teaspoon dry mustard
1/2 teaspoon celery seed
1/4 teaspoon cayenne pepper

In a small bowl combine oil, margarine, onion and garlic. Cook on HIGH for 3-4 minutes until tender. Add remaining ingredients, stir, and cook on HIGH for 3-4 minutes, stirring again during cooking time.

Creamy Tomato Sauce

Attractive poured over fish fillets and steamed greens.

1 clove garlic, minced
2 green onions, thinly chopped
2 teaspoons olive oil
2 teaspoons margarine
1 large chopped tomato or 1 cup drained, chopped canned tomatoes
1/8 teaspoon dried tarragon
2 Tablespoons fat-free plain yogurt
1/4 teaspoon lemon-pepper seasoning

In a small bowl, combine garlic, onion, oil, and margarine. Microwave on HIGH for 1 minute. Stir in remaining ingredients and microwave on HIGH for 1-2 minutes until heated through, stirring once.

Cranberry-Orange Sauce

yields 2 cups

Good with turkey, chicken or game hens.

> **1 (2-ounce) package frozen unsweetened cranberries**
> **1/4 cup orange juice**
> **1/2 cup honey**

Combine all ingredients in a 2-quart casserole dish. Cover with wax paper and microwave on MEDIUM (50% power) for 8-12 minutes until berry skins have popped, stirring twice.

Lite Hollandaise Sauce

yields 2/3 cup

> **1/2 cup low-fat mayonnaise or mayonnaise substitute**
> **2 Tablespoons water**
> **1 Tablespoon lemon juice**
> **1 Tablespoon margarine**
> **dash cayenne pepper**
> **1/2 teaspoon dried tarragon**

Whisk together all ingredients in a small bowl. Microwave on MEDIUM (50% power) for 1 1/2 minutes until warm.

Mushroom Gravy

Use as a substitute for traditional gravy. Pour over potatoes, rice, vegetables and meat.

> **1 1/4 cups water**
> **2 teaspoons cornstarch**

8 ounces fresh sliced mushrooms
1/8 cup finely chopped onion
1 teaspoon low-salt beef bouillon granules
1/8 teaspoon coarse ground black pepper
1/2 teaspoon dried basil
1/4 teaspoon garlic powder
1/4 teaspoon onion powder
dash cayenne pepper

Pour water and cornstarch into a 1 1/2-quart casserole dish, stir well. Add remaining ingredients. Cover and microwave on HIGH 3-6 minutes until mushrooms are soft, and sauce is transparent and beginning to thicken.

Peach Chutney

yields 2 cups

1 clove garlic, minced
1/2 teaspoon ground ginger
2 Tablespoons cider vinegar
1/4 cup honey
2 pounds fresh ripe peaches, coarsely chopped
1/2 cup pitted, chopped dates
1 teaspoon fresh lime or lemon juice
2 teaspoons Dijon mustard
1/4 teaspoon salt
1/8 teaspoon cayenne pepper

In a small bowl, combine garlic, ginger, vinegar and honey. Cover with wax paper and microwave on HIGH for 3 minutes, stirring once.

Stir in remaining ingredients. Recover and microwave on HIGH for 6-8 minutes, stirring once halfway through cooking time. Refrigerate for up to one week.

Mushroom and Green Onion Pate

yields 2 cups

Mouth watering on grilled garlic bread.

> 1 Tablespoon olive oil
> 1/2 cup finely chopped green onion
> 1 pound fresh mushrooms, sliced
> 2 Tablespoons red wine
> 1 teaspoon salt-free seasoning
> 1/2 cup plain fat-free yogurt
> 1/2 cup chopped walnuts

In a 2 1/2-quart casserole dish, combine oil and onion. Microwave on HIGH for 2 minutes. Stir in mushrooms, leave uncovered, and cook on HIGH for 5-6 minutes until mushrooms are tender.

Pour mushroom mixture into container of blender or food processor. Add remaining ingredients, except nuts, and puree. Fold in nuts. Transfer to serving bowl and chill for 3 hours.

Red and Green Bell Pepper Cheese Mold

Yields 2 cups

Delectable spread on Italian bread.

> 3 Tablespoons water
> 1 packet unflavored gelatin
> 1 (15-ounce) container low-fat ricotta cheese
> 1/2 cup red bell pepper, finely chopped
> 1/4 cup green bell pepper, finely chopped
> 1/2 cup green onions, finely chopped
> 1/2 cup plain fat-free yogurt
> 1 Tablespoon lemon juice
> 1/4 teaspoon salt

Combine water and gelatin in medium bowl. Microwave on HIGH for 45 seconds to dissolve gelatin, stirring twice.

Stir in remaining ingredients. Line a 2-cup form or bowl with plastic wrap and fill with cheese mixture. Cover and refrigerate from 3 hours to overnight.

To serve, unmold onto serving plate and remove plastic wrap.

Nut Bread Spread

Wonderful with fresh baked banana nut bread.

Yields 1 cup

> 1 (8-ounce) package low-fat cream cheese
> 1 teaspoon grated lemon rind
> 3 Tablespoons maple syrup
> 1/2 teaspoon ground cinnamon

Unwrap cream cheese and place in a bowl. Microwave on MEDIUM LOW (30% power) for 1-2 minutes to soften. Blend in remaining ingredients. Spoon into serving dish and refrigerate until serving time.

Bacon and Mushroom Baked Potato Topping

serves 2

> 2 slices turkey bacon, chopped
> 1 shallot, minced
> 2 Tablespoons chopped green onion
> 4-5 medium mushrooms, chopped
> 2 teaspoons margarine

Place turkey bacon on plate and microwave on HIGH for 3-4 minutes until crisp. Set bacon aside.

Place shallot, onion, mushrooms, and margarine into a casserole dish. Cover and microwave on HIGH for 2 minutes, until shallots are tender-crisp, stirring once.

Crumble bacon into mixture and spoon over hot, split baked potatoes.

Creamy Onion and Pea Baked Potato Topping

serves 2

> 1/4 cup frozen peas, thawed
> 1/4 cup diced green onion
> 1/2 cup plain low-fat yogurt
> 2 Tablespoons grated Parmesan cheese

Place peas and onion in measuring cup and microwave on HIGH for 1-2 minutes to heat. Add yogurt and stir. Spoon over hot split potatoes and sprinkle with Parmesan cheese.

Pureed Eggplant Dip

Use as a dip with torn, whole wheat pitas.

> 1 1/2 pounds eggplant
> 1 Tablespoon olive oil
> 1 Tablespoon fresh lemon juice
> 1 clove garlic, crushed
> 1 teaspoon salt-free seasoning
> 2 Tablespoons green onions, diced

Pierce eggplant with a knife in several places. Set on a double layer of paper towels in the oven and cook on HIGH for 9-11 minutes. Allow to cool.

Cut eggplant in half lengthwise. Spoon out flesh and place in the container of a blender. Add remaining ingredients and puree. Transfer to serving bowl.

Clam and Cheese Dip

> 1/2 package lite cream cheese (4-ounce)
> 1 (6 1/2-ounce) can drained minced clams
> 1/4 cup plain low-fat yogurt
> 1 clove minced garlic
> 1 teaspoon Worcestershire sauce
> 1 Tablespoon fresh cilantro leaves

Place cheese in medium bowl. Microwave on MEDIUM (50% power) for 1 minute to soften cheese.

Mix in remaining ingredients. Microwave on MEDIUM for 3-5 minutes more minutes to heat throughout, stirring after half the cooking time.

Red Pepper Dip

A beautiful condiment with simply cooked fish and chicken. Add to soups.

Yields 2 cups

> 2 red bell peppers, seeded and coarsely chopped
> 2 teaspoons capers, drained and rinsed
> dash black pepper

Place bell peppers in a 2-quart casserole dish. Cover and cook on HIGH for 4-6 minutes until tender.

Place cooked peppers, capers and black pepper in container of blender. Puree.

Broccoli Dip

yields 2 cups

> 3/4 pound broccoli, trimmed, coarsely chopped
> 3/4 cup low-salt chicken broth
> 1 cup part-skim ricotta cheese
> 1 teaspoon ground cumin
> 1 teaspoon salt-free seasoning
> dash black pepper

Combine broccoli and chicken broth in a 2 1/2-quart casserole dish. Cover and cook on HIGH for 4-5 minutes until broccoli is fork-tender.

While broccoli is cooking, puree ricotta in a blender until smooth. When broccoli is cooked, add to ricotta in blender container along with seasonings. Puree until smooth.

Onion and Shallot Sauce

yields 2 cups

2 Tablespoons olive oil
2 medium red onions, sliced thin, rings separated
4 green onions, diced
4 shallots, diced
1/2 cup dry white wine
1 Tablespoon honey
1 teaspoon salt-free seasoning
dash black pepper

In a 2 1/2-quart casserole dish, combine olive oil, red onions, green onions and shallots. Cover and microwave on HIGH for 3-5 minutes until onions are tender.

Stir in wine, honey, seasoning and pepper. Cover and microwave on MEDIUM HIGH (70% power) for 3-4 minutes until hot through and flavors have blended. Let stand 10 minutes.

Apple-Cranberry Sauce

1 cup fresh or thawed frozen cranberries
1 small apple, cored and chopped
1/4 cup apple juice
1/2 teaspoon ground cinnamon
1 Tablespoon honey

In a 1 1/2-quart casserole dish, combine all ingredients. Microwave on HIGH for 3-4 minutes until cranberry skins pop, stirring twice. Allow to cool. Cover and refrigerate until serving time.

Warm Vinaigrette with Bacon Bits

> 2 slices turkey bacon, chopped
> 2 Tablespoons olive oil
> 1 Tablespoon fresh lemon juice
> 1 Tablespoon red wine vinegar
> 2 teaspoons honey
> 1/2 teaspoon salt-free seasoning
> dash black pepper

Arrange turkey bacon on a paper plate, cover with a paper towel, and microwave on HIGH for 2-3 minutes until slightly crispy.

In a medium bowl, whisk together bacon and remainder of ingredients. Microwave on HIGH for 1 minute. Toss on salad greens while still warm.

Tomato Sautéed Onions and Pepper

yields 2 cups.

Try as a condiment with cooked meats instead of catsup.

> 2 Tablespoons diced bell pepper
> 1 large onion, sliced, rings separated
> 2/3 cup canned, low-salt stewed tomatoes
> 1/2 Tablespoons tomato paste
> 1 Tablespoon red wine vinegar
> 1/2 teaspoon honey

Combine all ingredients in a 2 1/2-quart casserole dish. Cover and cook on HIGH for 4-6 minutes until onions are tender, stirring twice. Serve hot or chilled.

Green Salsa

yields about 1 1/2 cups

> **1/2 pound tomatillos, husks removed, cored and coarsely chopped**
> **1/4 cup chopped onion**
> **1 fresh jalapeño pepper diced, or 1 (4-ounce) can diced green chiles**
> **1 large clove garlic, crushed**
> **1 Tablespoon canola oil, or other vegetable oil**

Combine tomatillos, onion, pepper and garlic in a 2-quart casserole dish. Cover and cook on HIGH for 2 minutes until tender-crisp. Stir in remaining ingredients. Refrigerate until ready to serve.

Tomato and Black Olive Sauce for Fish

> **3 cloves garlic, minced**
> **2 teaspoons olive oil**
> **1/4 cup diced green onion**
> **1/4 cup diced zucchini**
> **2 medium tomatoes, seeded and chopped**
> **1/2 teaspoon dried basil**
> **dash cayenne pepper**
> **1 (3-ounce) can ripe pitted olives, drained and chopped**
> **4 teaspoons capers, drained**

In a 1 1/2-quart casserole dish, combine garlic, oil, onion and zucchini. Microwave on HIGH for 1 1/2 minutes until tender crisp.

Stir in remaining ingredients. Microwave on HIGH for 2 minutes. Let stand 20 minutes to allow flavors to blend and to cool to room temperature.

Mushroom Sauce

Makes simply cooked rice and noodles something special.

12 ounces fresh mushrooms, coarsely chopped
1 cup chicken broth
2 teaspoons olive oil
1/2 teaspoon salt-free seasoning
dash black pepper

Place all ingredients in a 2 1/2-quart casserole dish. Cover and microwave on HIGH for 5-6 minutes until mushrooms are soft, stirring once.

Transfer to blender and puree.

Dill Tartar Sauce

yields 1 cup

2/3 cup fat-free plain yogurt
1/3 cup low—fat mayonnaise or mayonnaise substitute
2 Tablespoons diced dill pickle
1/2 teaspoon onion powder

Combine all ingredients in a small bowl. Cover and refrigerate for at least 2 hours to allow flavors to blend.

Cheese and Onion Potato Topping

yields 3/4 cup

1 small onion, thinly sliced, rings separated
2 teaspoons olive oil
1 teaspoon salt-free seasoning
1/4 cup fat-free plain yogurt
1/4 cup shredded, fat-free Cheddar cheese

Combine oil and onion in a 2-quart casserole dish. Cover and cook on HIGH for 2-3 minutes until tender.

Stir in seasoning, yogurt and cheese. Reduce heat to MEDIUM (50% power). Cover and microwave for 2-3 minutes, stirring twice, to heat through. Serve over hot slit baked potatoes.

Hearty Italian Potato Topping

1/2 pound ground turkey
1/4 cup chopped onion
2 cups spaghetti sauce
1 teaspoon parsley flakes, for garnish

Combine turkey and onion in a microwaveable colander. Place colander in bowl. Microwave on HIGH for 3-4 minutes until meat is no longer pink, stirring twice to break apart meat.

In a medium sized bowl, combine spaghetti sauce with turkey-onion mixture. Cover and microwave on HIGH for 3-4 minutes to heat through.

Spoon spaghetti sauce mixture over hot slit baked potatoes and sprinkle with parsley flakes.

Yogurt Dill Potato Topping

yields about 3/4 cup

1 large clove garlic, crushed or minced
1 Tablespoon water
3/4 cup plain fat-free yogurt
2 Tablespoons fresh dill chopped, or 1 teaspoon dried dill
1 teaspoon fresh lemon juice
1/8 teaspoon salt
1/8 teaspoon black pepper

Place water and garlic in a 2-cup microwaveable measure. Cover with plastic wrap. Microwave on HIGH for 1 minute.

Add remaining ingredients and stir.

Shrimp Potato Topping

> 1 cup sliced mushrooms
> 1 teaspoon olive oil
> 1/2 teaspoon salt-free seasoning
> 1/3 cup plain fat-free yogurt
> 1/2 pound medium shrimp, shelled and de-veined
> 2 teaspoons chopped parsley

Combine all ingredients in a 2-quart casserole dish. Cover and microwave on MEDIUM (50% power) for 6-8 minutes, stirring twice. Serve over hot slit potatoes.

Neufchatel and Bell Pepper Potato Topping

> 2 teaspoons olive oil
> 2 Tablespoons minced red bell pepper
> 2 Tablespoons minced green bell pepper
> 2 cloves garlic, minced
> dash onion salt
> dash black pepper
> 2 ounces Neufchatel cheese

In a baking dish, microwave oil, peppers, and garlic on HIGH for 2 minutes until vegetables are tender-crisp. Season with salt and pepper.

Spoon cheese onto hot split potatoes and microwave on HIGH for 1 minute. Top with bell pepper mixture.

181

DESSERTS

Apple Crisp

3 cups cored, peeled, sliced apples
1 Tablespoon honey
1 teaspoon fresh lemon juice

Topping
1/4 cup whole wheat flour
1/4 cup wheat germ or toasted bran
1/8 cup lightly packed brown sugar
1 teaspoon ground cinnamon
2 teaspoons margarine

Mix apples, honey and lemon in an 8-inch baking dish. Combine topping ingredients in a bowl, cutting in margarine with 2 knives. Sprinkle topping mixture over apples in an even layer. Microwave on HIGH for 7-10 minutes until apples are tender, rotating dish every 4 minutes. Serve warm.

Oranges and Kiwi in Sweet Juice

4 ripe kiwi, peeled and sliced
2 oranges, peeled and sectioned
1 Tablespoon fresh lemon juice
1/4 cup orange juice
2 Tablespoons honey
2 Tablespoons chopped walnuts

Arrange kiwi and orange sections in individual serving bowls. In 2-cup measure, stir lemon juice, orange juice and honey. Microwave on HIGH for 1-2 minutes to thin honey. Stir and pour over fruit. Garnish with chopped nuts.

Pear and Date Compote

1/2 cup fresh squeezed orange juice
2 Tablespoons honey
3 pears, cored, peeled and sliced
1/3 cup dates, chopped
1/2 teaspoon ground cinnamon
3 Tablespoons sesame seeds

In 2-cup measure, combine orange juice and honey and microwave on HIGH for 1-2 minutes to thin honey. Stir.

In casserole dish combine juice mixture, pears, dates, and cinnamon. Cover and microwave on HIGH for 4-6 minutes until pears are tender, stirring twice. Garnish with sesame seeds.

Basic Whole Wheat Bread Crumbs

yields about 1 1/2 cups

5 slices of leftover whole wheat bread, torn into pieces

Put bread into bowl of food processor and pulse until you have crumbs.

Place crumbs in a pie plate and cook, uncovered, on HIGH for 4-5 minutes, until completely dried, stirring twice.

Honeydew with Lime and Mint

2 teaspoons honey
2 Tablespoons fresh lime juice
1 Tablespoon fresh chopped mint or teaspoon dried
1 honeydew melon (3 pounds) peeled, seeded, cut into 1-inch cubes.

Combine honey, lime juice and mint in a small bowl. Microwave on HIGH for 45 seconds to thin honey. Place melon into a large serving bowl and drizzle lemon mixture on top.

Raisin Noodle Pudding

> 1/3 pound hot cooked eggless noodles, medium width, drained (about 5 cups)
> 1 Tablespoons margarine
> 4 egg whites
> 6 ounces low-fat cottage cheese
> 1/2 cup plain fat-free yogurt
> 1/4 cup honey
> 1 teaspoon cinnamon
> 1 teaspoon vanilla extract
> 1 cup raisins
> 1/4 teaspoon nutmeg, for garnish.

Place hot noodles in a bowl and add margarine, allowing it to melt.

In a large bowl, beat egg whites and cottage cheese together until smooth. Stir in yogurt, honey, cinnamon, vanilla and raisins.

Pour noodle mixture into a 2-quart casserole dish. Sprinkle with nutmeg. Leave uncovered and microwave on HIGH for 13-15 minutes until just set, rotating dish every 5 minutes. Let stand for 5 minutes.

Cooked Strawberries and Rhubarb

Strawberry Sauce

yields 1 1/2 cups

Have some over puddings, pancakes, French toast or frozen yogurt.

> 1 Tablespoon cornstarch
> 1 1/2 Tablespoons sugar
> 1/2 cup cranberry juice
> 1 cup fresh, or frozen, thawed, strawberries, sliced

In a bowl, combine cornstarch, sugar and cranberry juice. Stir in strawberries. Cook on HIGH for 2 1/2-3 minutes until sauce is thickened, stirring each 1 minute.

2 cups fresh rhubarb, cut into 1-inch pieces
6 fresh strawberries, trimmed, sliced in half
3 Tablespoons honey

Place rhubarb and strawberries in a 2-quart casserole dish. Cover and cook on HIGH for 4-5 minutes until rhubarb is completely soft. Stir in honey. Let stand 5 minutes.

Gingered Strawberries

1 pint fresh strawberries, hulled and quartered
1 teaspoon peeled and grated fresh ginger

Toss ingredients together in a medium size bowl. Chill until serving.

Strawberries and 'Cream'

1/4 cup cranberry juice
3 teaspoons unflavored gelatin
3/4 pound strawberries, trimmed
2 Tablespoons honey
1/2 cup part-skim ricotta cheese
4 strawberries, for garnish

Combine juice and gelatin in a small bowl. Let stand 1 minute. Microwave uncovered on HIGH for 1 minute. Set aside. Puree strawberries, honey, and ricotta in a blender. Blend in dissolved gelatin. Pour into individual dessert cups, garnish with whole strawberry, and chill for 1-2 hours.

Frozen Banana Shake

yields about 2 1/2 cups

Better than ice cream.

> 1 cup orange juice (may substitute pineapple juice,
>   apple juice, tropical juice)
> 1 medium size frozen banana, broken into 1-inch
>   pieces
> 1 large ripe peach, peeled and sliced (may substitute
>   nectarine, mango, cantaloupe)

Place all ingredients in the container of a blender. Blend a few seconds until smooth.

Bananas with Kalua and 'Cream'

> 1/4 cup plain fat-free yogurt
> 1 Tablespoon Kalua
> 4 small peeled bananas, sliced into uniformly sized
>   coins

Mix together yogurt and Kalua in a small bowl. Microwave on MEDIUM (50% power) for 1 minute to heat through.

Place bananas in a round 1-quart casserole dish and pour yogurt mixture over top. Gently toss. Microwave on HIGH for 1 minute until hot. Divide into individual dessert plates.

Creamy Rice Pudding

> 1 cup short grain white rice
> 3 1/2 cups non-fat milk, divided
> 1/2 teaspoon cinnamon, divided
> 1 1/2 Tablespoons honey
> 1 teaspoon vanilla extract
> 3 Tablespoons raisins
> 1/4 cup plain fat-free yogurt

Combine rice and 1 cup milk in a 2 1/2-quart casserole dish. Cover and cook on HIGH for 3 minutes until almost boiling.

Stir in 1 cup milk, 1/4 teaspoon cinnamon, honey and vanilla. Cover and microwave on MEDIUM (50% power) for 8 minutes. Stir in 1 cup of milk, and raisins, Re-cover and cook an additional 8 minutes on MEDIUM. Stir in last 1/2 cup of milk. Re-cover and cook on MEDIUM for 4 minutes.

Let stand, covered for 30 minutes until most of the liquid is absorbed. Stir in yogurt. Sprinkle with remaining cinnamon.

Peppered Oranges

4 juice oranges
dash freshly ground black pepper

Peel oranges. Cut crosswise 1/2-inch thick and remove seeds. Arrange overlapping on a plate and sprinkle very lightly with pepper.

Grapefruit and Maple Ice

yields 4 scoops

Serve this desert alone, or surround with grapes, orange segments and sliced bananas.

2 ripe grapefruit, peeled, segmented, seeds and membranes removed
2 Tablespoons maple syrup
Cinnamon to taste

Place grapefruit segments in an even layer on a microwaveable dish. Freeze until solid, 4 hours or overnight. Place dish in oven and microwave on MEDIUM LOW (30% power) for 1-2 minutes—just long enough to break apart pieces. Place grapefruit and maple syrup in container of a food processor and process until smooth. Spoon into bowls and sprinkle with cinnamon.

Tapioca Pudding

>   1 1/2 Tablespoons honey
>   2 cups skim milk
>   3 Tablespoons instant tapioca
>   1/4 cup liquid egg substitute
>   1 teaspoon vanilla

Place honey in a 2-quart casserole dish and microwave on HIGH for 45 seconds to thin. Stir in milk and tapioca.

Cover and cook on HIGH for 3 minutes. Stir. Leave uncovered and cook on HIGH another 3 minutes, stirring every 1 minute.

In a small bowl, beat together egg substitute and vanilla. Slowly stir 1/2 cup of the hot tapioca mixture into the eggs to equalize temperatures. Slowly stir egg mixture back into tapioca. Leave uncovered. Microwave on HIGH for 1 minute.

Stir. Let stand 20 minutes. If desired, cover surface of tapioca with plastic wrap to prevent skin from forming. Serve warm or chilled.

Carob Mint Tapioca Pudding

Carob powder, made from ground pods of the carob tree, has the look and taste of chocolate, but without the caffeine. It is available in health food stores.

>   1 1/2 Tablespoons honey
>   2 cups skim milk, divided
>   2 Tablespoons carob powder
>   3 Tablespoons instant tapioca
>   2 egg whites
>   1 teaspoon vanilla extract
>   2 drops spearmint extract
>   4 mint leaves for garnish

Place honey and 1/2 cup milk in a 2-quart casserole dish and microwave on HIGH for 1 minute to thin honey and heat milk. Sprinkle carob powder on top and let stand 1 minute. Mix together to form a smooth paste.

Add remainder of the milk and the tapioca. Cover and cook on HIGH for 3 minutes. Leave uncovered and cook on HIGH an additional 3 minutes, stirring each one minute.

Beat together egg whites, vanilla, and mint extract. Slowly stir 1/2 cup of the hot tapioca mixture into the egg mixture to equalize temperatures. Slowly stir egg mixture back into the tapioca mixture. Cook on HIGH for 1 minute, leaving uncovered

Stir. Let stand 20 minutes. If desired, cover surface of tapioca with plastic wrap to prevent skin from forming. Serve warm or chilled. Garnish with fresh mint leaves.

Pineapple and Strawberry Tapioca Pudding

1 1/2 Tablespoons honey
2 cups unsweetened pineapple juice
3 Tablespoons instant tapioca
8 sliced strawberries, for garnish

Place honey in a 2-quart casserole dish and microwave on HIGH for 45 seconds to thin. Stir in juice and tapioca. Let stand 5 minutes.

Cover and cook on HIGH for 3 minutes. Stir well. Leave uncovered, and cook on HIGH another 3 minutes, stirring each one minute.

Stir. Let stand 20 minutes. If desired, cover surface of tapioca with microwaveable plastic wrap to prevent skin from forming. Serve warm or chilled. Before serving, garnish with fresh strawberries.

Special Bread Pudding

serves 6

> 1 1/2 cup apple juice
> 1 Tablespoon honey
> 1/2 cup raisins
> 1/4 cup liquid egg substitute
> 1/2 teaspoon vanilla
> 5 slices firm whole wheat bread, cubed
> 3 Tablespoons chopped walnuts

Combine juice, honey and raisins in a bowl and cook on high for 2 minutes. Allow to cool a few minutes. Whisk egg substitute and vanilla in a small bowl. Slowly blend a bit of juice mixture into egg mixture, allowing temperatures to equalize. Slowly blend all egg mixture back into juice mixture.

In a 2-quart casserole dish, arrange layers of bread cubes, raisin mixture and walnuts. Pour egg/juice mixture over bread. Make sure all bread pieces are dampened by juice mixture. Cover with wax paper and microwave on HIGH for 3-5 minutes until set. Serve hot or cold.

Spiced Pears with Glaze

Enjoy pears alone or with a scoop of frozen nonfat yogurt.

> 2 large fresh ripe pears, core removed
> 1/4 cup apple juice
> 1 Tablespoon lemon juice
> 1/4 cup dry white wine
> 2 Tablespoons honey
> 1/2 teaspoon vanilla extract
> 2 Tablespoons raisins
> 1/4 teaspoon ground cinnamon
> 1/8 teaspoon ground nutmeg
> 1 teaspoon cornstarch

Cut pears in half lengthwise and pierce each half with fork. Place cut side up in 8 x 5-inch baking dish.

Combine remaining ingredients in a small bowl. Microwave on HIGH 2-3 minutes, or until thickened, stirring twice. Pour glaze over pears and cover with wax paper. Microwave on HIGH for 7-9 minutes until tender, rearranging and basting with glaze once. Let stand 3 minutes. Serve warm with sauce.

Baked Apples

> 4 medium apples
> 1/3 cup apple juice
> 1/4 cup raisins
> 1/2 teaspoon ground cinnamon

Core apples, being careful not to cut through bottoms. Place in custard cups. Pour apple juice, raisins and cinnamon into each apple. Cover loosely with plastic wrap. Microwave on HIGH for 7-9 minutes until apples are fork-tender, rearranging and rotating after half the time. Let stand 2 minutes. Serve warm.

Warm Fruit Medley

> 2 large oranges, peeled and sectioned
> 1/4 cup seedless grapes
> 1/4 cup fresh strawberries, halved
> 2 medium bananas, sliced into 1/2-inch pieces
> 1/4 cup apple juice
> 1/4 teaspoon cinnamon

Divide fruit evenly into 4 custard cups. Pour an equal amount of apple juice over each. Sprinkle with cinnamon. Cover with wax paper and cook on HIGH for 3-4 minutes until bananas begin to soften, rotating once during cooking time. Serve warm.

Coconut Covered Chocolate Banana Splits

> 1/2 cup coconut flakes
> 8 small scoops fat-free chocolate frozen yogurt
> 2 bananas, peeled, cut in half crosswise, each half
>   sliced in 4 strips

Spread out coconut on wax paper. Roll frozen yogurt scoops in coconut. Place on baking sheet and place in freezer.

Arrange 4 banana strips in bottoms of 4 serving dishes. Top with 2 scoops coconut covered frozen yogurt.

Fresh Berries with Yogurt and Mint

> 3 cups fully ripe berries (strawberries, raspberries,
>   blueberries, or a mixture)
> 1 (8-ounce) container vanilla fat-free yogurt, stirred
> 8-12 fresh mint leaves for garnish

Just before serving, rinse berries and divide among 4 dessert bowls. Top with yogurt and a few mint leaves.

Dried and Fresh Fruit Compote

> 5 ounces pitted prunes
> 6 ounces dried apricots
> 2 cups orange juice
> 2 oranges, peeled and sectioned
> 1 banana, sliced
> 1 cup seedless grapes

Pour dried fruit and orange juice into a medium bowl. Cover and marinate for 6-10 hours.

Pour marinated fruit, oranges, bananas and grapes into casserole dish; stir. Cook on HIGH for 4-6 minutes until fruit is softened and hot throughout. Serve hot or cold.

Cinnamon Dusted Chocolate Frozen Yogurt Balls with 'Cream'

Easy but elegant.

> 1/2 cup vanilla low-fat yogurt
> 8 small scoops chocolate low-fat frozen yogurt
> 1/2-1 teaspoon ground cinnamon

Stir in vanilla yogurt and spoon 2 Tablespoons onto 4 dessert plates. Top with 2 scoops chocolate yogurt. Sprinkle with cinnamon.

Apple Tasting and Cheddar Cheese

> 1 McIntosh apple, sliced into 1/2-inch wedges
> 1 Red Delicious apple, sliced into 1/2-inch wedges
> 1 Granny Smith apple, sliced into 1/2-inch wedges
> 2 ounces low-fat Cheddar cheese, sliced

Arrange apple wedges and cheese on serving platter and enjoy comparing flavors.

Warm Pear Slices with Yogurt and Berries

4 firm ripe pears, peeled, core removed, sliced into 1/4-inch slices
1/3 cup apple juice
1/2 teaspoon ground cinnamon
1/2 cup fat-free vanilla yogurt
1/2 cup fresh berries (blueberries, strawberries)

In a 2 1/2-quart casserole dish, combine pears, apple juice, and cinnamon. Cover and microwave on HIGH for 6-8 minutes until pears are tender but not mushy, stirring gently once. Chill in liquid until serving time.

To serve, spoon pears and sauce onto dessert plates. Top with a dollop of yogurt and sprinkle with berries.

Peach Sorbet

yields 4 large scoops

Enjoy this sorbet on its own, or top with chunks of cantaloupe, and strawberries.

3/4 pound fresh ripe peaches, peeled, pitted and sliced
1 Tablespoon honey
1/4 cup fat-free vanilla yogurt
dash ground nutmeg for garnish

Place peaches in single layer on microwaveable dish and cook on MEDIUM LOW (30% power) for 1-2 minutes until you can just break apart pieces. Place peaches in food processor and process until finely chopped. Add remaining ingredients except nutmeg and process until mixture is creamy. Scoop into bowls and sprinkle with nutmeg.

Cooked Apples A La Mode

An easy alternative to apple pie.

> 1 Tablespoon margarine
> 1/8 cup maple syrup
> 1/4 cup apple juice
> 1 teaspoon lemon juice
> 2 large cooking apples, peeled, cored, cut into 1/4-inch
>   slices
> 4-8 scoops low-fat vanilla ice cream
> 1/2 teaspoon ground cinnamon for garnish

In a glass pie plate, heat margarine on HIGH for 15 seconds to melt. Stir in syrup, and apple and lemon juices. Add apples and coat well. Cover with wax paper and microwave on HIGH for 6-8 minutes until apples are tender.

Scoop ice cream into serving bowls and spoon apple mixture and juice on top. Sprinkle with cinnamon.

Pumpkin Custard

serves 6

An autumn favorite

> 1 Tablespoon margarine
> 1 pound seeded, peeled pumpkin, cut into cubes
> 1/2 cup liquid egg substitute, beaten
> 1/4 cup slightly packed brown sugar
> 1/4 cup fat-free yogurt
> 1 teaspoon vanilla
> 1/4 teaspoon ground cinnamon, for garnish
> dash nutmeg, for garnish

Combine margarine and pumpkin in a glass pie plate. Cover with wax paper and microwave on HIGH for 6-8 minutes until tender, stirring once. Meanwhile, combine remaining ingredients, except cinnamon and nutmeg, in a medium bowl. Set aside.

Place cooked pumpkin in container of blender or food processor and puree. Fold into egg sugar mixture. Pour back into pie plate, sprinkle with cinnamon and nutmeg and microwave uncovered on MEDIUM (50% power) for 12-14 minutes until just set, rotating 3 times. Let stand 10 minutes.

Warm Pineapple Slices with Raspberry Sherbet

> **2 Tablespoons maple syrup**
> **1 cup fresh pineapple chunks or canned chunks, drained**
> **1/4 teaspoon cinnamon**
> **1 (11-ounce) can mandarin orange sections packed in juice, or 1 cup freshorange sections**
> **1 pint raspberry sherbet**

Drain canned pineapple and orange pieces. In 1 1/2-quart casserole dish, combine fruit with maple syrup and cinnamon. Cover with wax paper and microwave on HIGH for 1-2 minutes until heated through, stirring once. Spoon into individual serving dishes and top with a scoop of sherbet.

SNACKS/DRINKS

Wine Warmer

> 2 cups dry white wine
> 1 cup orange juice
> 1 cup pineapple juice
> 8 orange segments
> 4 cinnamon sticks
> 1/4 teaspoon cinnamon

In 2-quart casserole dish, combine all ingredients except cinnamon sticks. Cover and microwave on HIGH for 7-9 minutes until boiling, stirring once. Pour into mugs and insert cinnamon sticks as stirrers.

Spiced Indian Tea

> 4 cups water
> 1 strip of orange peel, 2 x 1/2-inch long
> 1 strip of lemon peel, 2 x 1/2-inch long
> 1 cinnamon stick
> 3 bags of black tea
> 1/2 cup low-fat milk
> honey to taste

Place the water in a microwaveable measure, cover with vented plastic wrap, and microwave on HIGH for 6-7 minutes until boiling. Add orange and lemon peel, cinnamon stick and tea. Let sleep for 5 minutes. Pour milk in a microwaveable measure and microwave on HIGH for 30-60 seconds until warm but not boiling.

Remove cinnamon, tea bags and citrus peels from tea and pour in serving container. Pour milk in serving container. Serve with honey on the side.

Garlic-Herb Popcorn

1 1/2 quarts popped corn
2 Tablespoons margarine
1/2 teaspoon garlic powder
1/4 teaspoon dried basil
1/4 teaspoon dried oregano

Using microwave popper, pop corn according to manufacturer's instructions. Pour popcorn into a large bowl. Place margarine in a small bowl and microwave on HIGH for 40-50 seconds. Blend in garlic powder and herbs and drizzle over popcorn.

Chicken-Zest Popcorn

1 1/2 quart popped corn
2 Tablespoons margarine
1/4 teaspoon chicken bouillon granules
1/2 teaspoon parsley flakes
1/8 teaspoon cayenne pepper

Using microwave popper, pop corn according to manufacturer's instructions. Pour popcorn into a large bowl. Place margarine in a small bowl and microwave on HIGH for 40-50 seconds. Blend in bouillon granules, parsley and cayenne pepper. Allow bouillon to dissolve. Drizzle over popcorn.

Homemade Tortilla Chips

6 (6-inch) corn tortillas, cut into pie shaped wedges
3 Tablespoons water
1/2 teaspoon lime juice

Pour water and lime juice into a cup. Stir. Brush tortilla wedges lightly with liquid. Place half the wedges on a microwaveable plate. Microwave on high for 3 minutes until crisp. Repeat with remaining wedges.

Raisin Apple Granola

yields about 2 1/2 cups

> **1 cup rolled oats**
> **1/4 cup chopped walnuts**
> **1/4 cup sunflower kernels**
> **2 Tablespoons bran**
> **2 Tablespoons wheat germ**
> **2 Tablespoons nonfat dry milk powder**
> **2 Tablespoons honey**
> **1 Tablespoon canola oil**
> **1/2 cup dried apples, chopped**
> **1/4 cup raisins**

In a baking dish, combine first 6 ingredients. Mix well.

In a 1-cup measure pour oil and swirl to coat. Add honey and microwave on HIGH for 45 seconds to thin honey.

Drizzle honey mixture over oat mixture, tossing to coat. Leave uncovered and microwave on HIGH for 2 minutes, stirring each 1 minute. Stir in apples and raisins and allow to cool, stirring occasionally.

Easy Nachos

> **3-4 cups Guiltless Gourmet tortilla chips**
> **1/2 cup vegetarian-style refried beans**
> **1 (4-ounce) can green chiles**
> **1/2 cup shredded low-fat Cheddar cheese**
> **1/2 Tablespoons taco seasoning, to garnish**

Place 1 layer of tortilla chips on 4 plates lined with paper towels. Top each with beans, chiles, cheese and a pinch of taco seasoning. Microwave each on HIGH for 1 minute until heated through and cheese melts.

Applesauce Raisin Muffins

yields 7

> 3/4 cup whole baking mix
> 1/4 teaspoon baking soda
> 1 Tablespoon brown sugar
> 1/2 teaspoon ground cinnamon
> 2 Tablespoons skim milk
> 1/3 cup unsweetened applesauce
> 1/4 cup liquid egg substitute (or 1 egg)
> 2 Tablespoons raisins
>
> Topping
> 2 teaspoons brown sugar
> 1 teaspoon ground cinnamon

Line 7 custard cups with paper baking cups.

In a small bowl, combine baking mix, baking soda, sugar, and cinnamon. Add milk, applesauce, egg and raisins. Stir well. Fill baking cups 1/2 full.

In another custard cup, mix together topping ingredients. Sprinkle on muffins. Arrange muffins in a ring in microwave oven and cook on HIGH for 1 minute.

Rotate cups 1/2 turn. Cook on HIGH another 1-2 minutes until tops bounce back when touched lightly. Remove immediately from custard cups to wire racks. Let cool.

Tomato and Green Chili on Whole Wheat Crackers

   3 medium tomatoes, chopped
   1 small onion, chopped
   2 Tablespoons canned green chiles, drained
   1 large clove garlic, crushed or minced
   1/2 teaspoon lemon juice
   1/2 teaspoon dried oregano
   1/2 teaspoon ground cumin
   12-16 whole wheat crackers
   1/4 cup shredded low-fat mozzarella cheese

Combine tomatoes, onion, chiles, garlic, and lemon juice in a
medium size bowl. Cook on HIGH for 5-6 minutes until
tomatoes are tender, stirring once. Drain. Add seasonings.

Top crackers with tomato mixture and arrange on a large
microwaveable platter. Sprinkle each with cheese to garnish.
Microwave on HIGH for 1 minute to melt cheese.

Quick Cracker Snack

   1 cup fat-free refried beans
   32 lowfat, low-salt whole wheat crackers
   1 medium tomato, sliced into cracker-size pieces
   1 small chili pepper, minced (serrano, jalapeño or
      Hungarian)

Place beans in a small bowl. Form a cavity in the center to allow
more even cooking. Microwave on HIGH for 1 1/2 - 2 minutes
until warm, stirring once.

Spread beans on crackers and top with tomato or tiny bits of
chili pepper.

Warmed Apple Cranberry Juice

   2 cups apple juice
   2 cups cranberry juice
   4 slices apple
   1 Tablespoon raisins
   4 cinnamon sticks

Combine all ingredients except cinnamon sticks in a 2-quart pouring bowl. Microwave on HIGH for 4-5 minutes until hot and fruit has softened.

Pour into mugs. Spoon some fruit into each. Add a cinnamon stick.

Mulled Cider

5 cups apple cider
1/2 teaspoon whole cloves
1/2 teaspoon whole allspice
4 cinnamon sticks

Combine all ingredients except cinnamon sticks in a medium size pouring bowl. Microwave on HIGH for 4-6 minutes until hot. Pour into large mugs and place one cinnamon stick in each.

Cafe au Lait

2 cups nonfat milk
2 cups water
1 1/2 Tablespoons Perro, Postum or other coffee
    substitute grain product
1 Tablespoon honey, optional
ground cinnamon, for garnish

Combine water and milk in a 2-quart casserole dish. Microwave on HIGH for 4-5 minutes until hot but not boiling. Stir in coffee substitute until dissolved. Add honey if desired. Pour into cups and sprinkle with cinnamon.

Hot Carob 'Cocoa'

serves 2

Carob is a natural substitute for cocoa. Powdered carob is available in health food stores.

> **1 Tablespoon carob powder**
> **2 cups skim milk**
> **2 teaspoons honey**
> **4 drops vanilla extract**

Place carob in a 4-cup microwaveable measure. Stir in just enough milk to make a smooth paste. Add remaining milk, honey and vanilla. Cover with plastic wrap and cook on HIGH for 2 1/2-3 minutes, stirring once. Pour into mugs to serve.

INDEX

COOKING CONVERSIONS

The metric unit for temperature is celsius.

Fahrenheit to Celsius =
Fahrenheit degree minus 32 times 5 divided by 9.

Celsius to Fahrenheit =
Celsius degree times 9 divided by 5 plus 32.

———————————

Whether you are working with liquid or dry
ingredients, the metric unit for volume is liters.
There are 1000 milliliters (ml) in one liter.

Starting with:	Multiply by:	To find:
teaspoons	5	# ml
Tablespoons	15	# ml
dry ounces	28	# ml
fluid ounces	30	# ml
cups	236	# ml

Volume		milliliters		fluid ounces
1/4 teaspoon	=	1.25	=	0.04
1/2 teaspoon	=	2.5	=	0.08
1 teaspoon	=	5	=	0.16 (1/6)
1/3 tablespoon	=	5	=	0.16 (1/6)
3 teaspoons	=	15	=	0.5 (1/2)
1 tablespoon	=	15	=	0.5 (1/2)
2 tablespoons	=	30	=	1
4 tablespoons	=	60	=	2
1/4 cup	=	60	=	2
8 tablespoons	=	120	=	4
1/2 cup	=	120	=	4
3/4 cup	=	180	=	6
1 cup	=	240	=	8
1 pint	=	480	=	16
1 quart	=	946	=	32
1 liter	=	1000	=	34
1 gallon	=	3.8 liters	=	128

Weight		grams		kilograms
0.035 ounce	=	1	=	0.001
1 ounce	=	28	=	0.028
4 ounces	=	112	=	0.112
1/4 pound	=	112	=	0.112
8 ounces	=	224	=	0.224
1/2 pound	=	224	=	0.224
16 ounces	=	448	=	0.45
1 pound	=	448	=	0.45